THE BORDER REIVERS

D1439747

THE
BORDER
REIVERS

GODFREY WATSON

**SANDHILL
PRESS**

First published in Great Britain by
Robert Hale & Company.
© Godfrey Watson 1974.
Reprinted 1985,1988, 1994 and 1998 by
Sandhill Press Ltd.,
17 Castle Street, Warkworth,
Northumberland NE65 0UW.

ISBN 0 946098 47 6

Cover design by Linda K. Graphic Design Studio,
Tel: (0191) 258 3464.

Printed in Great Britain by Martins the Printers Ltd.,
Berwick-upon-Tweed.

CONTENTS

ILLUSTRATIONS

MAPS

Credits.

The illustrations listed above were supplied by the following:
Numbers 1 to 23 and 26, 27 and 29 Peter Reynolds.
Numbers 24, 25 and 28 Hylton Edgar, Hexham.

ACKNOWLEDGEMENTS

My thanks are due to all those who have helped me in researching and producing this book. I have met with unfailing courtesy from the staffs of the Literary and Philosophical Society of Newcastle, the Newcastle Central Library, the National Library of Scotland and the Reading Room at the British Museum.

Without the willing assistance of Major Charlton of Hesleyside, Messrs Robson of the Hole Farm and the Vicar of Corbridge and Mr Iley, it would have been impossible to incorporate a number of the illustrations.

Above all, the help and encouragement of my wife, and the ability of Mary Bolton to read my writing, have made the book possible.

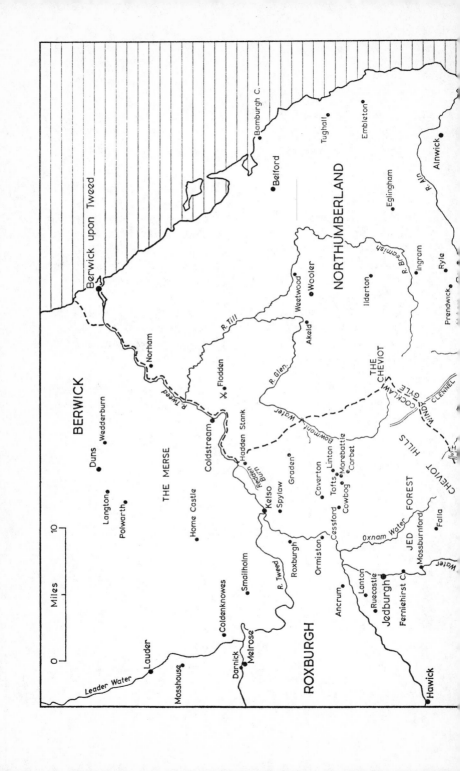

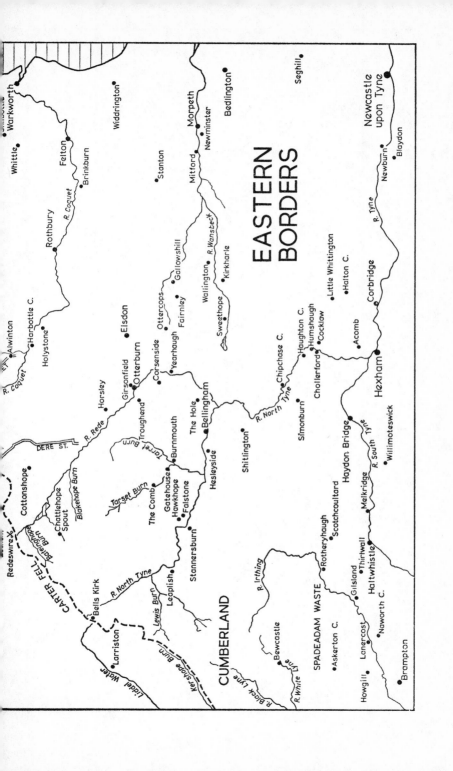

EASTERN
BORDERS

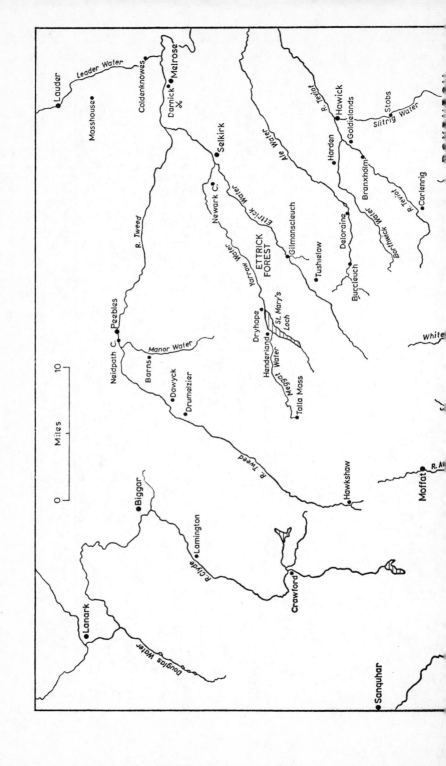

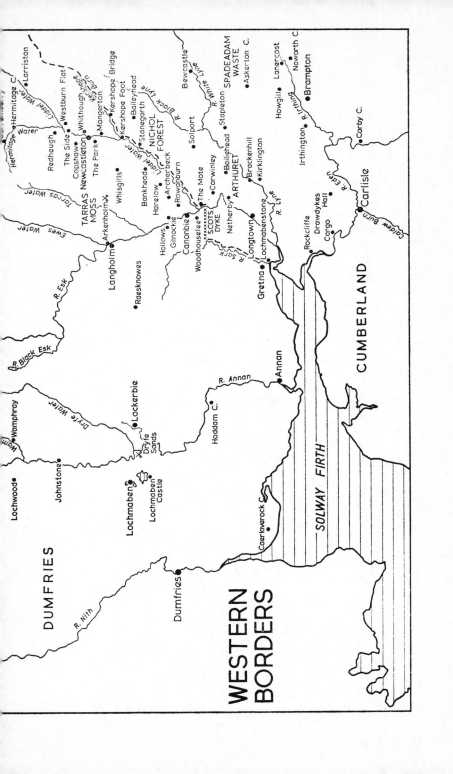

In memory of my Mother, whose love of the
Border Country I inherited

PREFACE

Scattered throughout the English-speaking world there must be hundreds of thousands, if not millions, of men and women in whose veins runs the blood of a class of men of whom they may never have heard. And not only this world; for was not the first man on the moon an Armstrong? There can, indeed, be few people of North Country or Lowland extraction who do not number among their progenitors Armstrongs, Elliots, Scotts, Bells, Nixons, Grahams, Routledges, Charltons, Robsons and others who were Border reivers; in other words men living in the countries on either side of the Border that separates Scotland from England, whose circumstances constrained them to earn a living by robbing and plundering others. Their heyday came between the end of the Scottish Wars of Independence and the Union of the two crowns, and more particularly during the sixteenth century with which this book is principally concerned. Though it is about the Border, it is in no way intended to be a history of all that went on there. Its purpose, in fact, is to try and explain to their descendants what kind of people the reivers really were and how they lived; perhaps even to explode some of the myths that have grown up around them.

At different times, and perhaps for different reasons, the Border reivers have been characterized as anything from jolly Knights Errant, robbing the rich to give to the poor, to a set of bloodthirsty scoundrels whose sole delight was in robbery and mayhem, without any kind of justification or even a redeeming feature. It is the author's hope that these pages will cast a little more light on a class of people who were not only interesting in themselves but who inspired the Border Ballads which form such a significant, if neglected, part of our literary heritage.

Having explained the intention behind the book, perhaps it

will not be out of place to add a word about the presentation. Where the ballads are quoted—and without them so much of the atmosphere would be lost—the spelling has not been altered except, of course, so far as Sir Walter Scott and others have imposed their own. On the other hand, where allusion is made to letters and documents of the period, the spelling, for the sake of clarity, is in the modern form except where the original presents no difficulty. Surnames, not unnaturally, pose a problem. Should Eure, for instance, appear as such, or as Evers? Should Ker be preferred to Kerr or Carr, as the name was so often spelt? In fact, the modern form is used unless there is good reason to the contrary.

CHAPTER ONE

Origin and Background

War appears to be as old as mankind, but peace is a modern
invention.   H. J. S. Maine

If, as has been suggested, Barabbas was a Borderer, who can
blame him? Who, indeed, can blame any frontier people,
exposed as they are to the territorial ambitions of both countries, if circumstances largely beyond their control force them
to indulge in robbery and violence? The tribes of the North-west
frontier of India were not the first and, even in these
enlightened days, are unlikely to be the last, whom politics
and the poverty dictated by unprofitable land have combined
to turn into a warlike race with respect for neither life nor
property.

    There was, indeed, little reason, originally, why those whose
lot it was to live on either side of what we now know as the
Border should have borne any natural enmity towards each
other. The Anglian kingdom of Northumbria had stretched not
only northwards towards the Tweed but, at one time, right up
to the Firth of Forth; while the Celtic kingdom of Strathclyde
included Cumberland. There was therefore an extensive inter-
mingling of peoples and an identity of outlook that was
increased, rather than otherwise, by the forced union of
Northumbria with Wessex, that left the North of England not
only rebellious but inward-looking. The later influx of a
Norman nobility into Scotland and the assimilation into that
country of prisoners taken in Northumberland, only served to
increase this identification. Northumberland itself as far as Newcastle, as well as those areas that subsequently became known
as North Durham, alternated for many years, both before and
after the Conquest, between Scotland and England, while

Scottish kings paid homage for Tynedale, off and on, until the end of the thirteenth century.

Both English and Scottish Borderers, then, sprang from much the same mixture of races, spoke much the same language (if with an increasingly different intonation) and shared much the same peculiarities. Yet the wars of aggression instigated by Edward I, and carried on by his successors, were to result in these people, with their similar civilizations and common interests, being set one against each other, and an artificial division imposed that was almost entirely foreign to them. As Robert Louis Stevenson put it: "Here are two people almost identical in blood . . . the same in language and religion; and yet a few years of quarrelsome isolation—in comparison with the great historical cycles—have so separated their thoughts and ways, that not unions nor mutual dangers, not steamers nor railways, nor all the king's horses and all the king's men seem able to obliterate the broad distinction."

Two and a half centuries of violent, if intermittent, warfare between England and Scotland were enough to reduce the Borders to a charred wilderness. When armies were not on the march, frontier raids were encouraged by both sides in order to wear down the enemy. So much so that, for centuries, men living within fifty miles of the Border could rarely go to sleep without the fear of attack. In other parts of the two countries the great barons had, throughout the Middle Ages, pursued their ends with fire and sword. It was only in the Borders that lesser men were virtually forced to imitate them.

As the years went by, things became worse rather than better. The people of Tynedale and Redesdale, like their neighbours in Scotland the more or less innocent victims of constant warfare, were left as often as not homeless and starving. "Scarce a soul", wrote a historian, "dared tc live in Northumberland unless it was near to some castle or walled town." The monks of Newminster suffered so much from the Scots' attacks on their flocks at Kidland, in the Cheviots, that they were forced to let the land to tenants who were at least capable of retaliation—a pastime that rapidly became a habit. The nuns of Holystone Priory, not far away, were so impoverished by Scottish raids that a special grant was made to them of the revenues of the churches of Holystone and Corsenside. Nor was the plight of those living north of the Cheviots any better.

Inevitably, the conditions under which the Borderers were forced to live, or rather to exist, led to impoverishment; and impoverishment led to violence. Perhaps in modern times the Black Market, together with more sophisticated forms of larceny, would have proved an acceptable alternative to starvation. However, for men whose sole wealth, for all practical purposes, lay in their herds of cattle and flocks of sheep, there was only one obvious answer, and that was to replenish their stocks from someone else's—a practice that may well have been suggested by their own tendency to hold their possessions in common.

In the Second World War there was a story current in North Africa that the French had persuaded those stealthy hillmen, the Goums, to steal up on the Germans in the dark, and cut their throats; payment being made for each ear supplied. It was only when it was discovered that there was little obvious difference between a German and an Allied ear that the exercise was reluctantly discontinued. Cattle, also, like cats, no doubt looked all the same in the dark, as Sir William Scott of Buccleuch was quick to point out when complaint was made to him by tenants who had suffered the loss of their herds, and he answered drily that "the Cumberland cattle were as good as those of Teviotdale". To many, however, England must have seemed a long way away and, once committed to robbery, it would be very tempting to turn one's attention to cattle that were nearer home. Nor were the Borderers on the English side backward in adopting a career which so neatly combined business and pleasure.

It might be imagined that great families such as the Percys and Nevilles, the Maxwells and Homes, with all the powers that their respective monarchs had encouraged them to amass, might have exerted some restraining influence on a situation that held in it all the seeds of anarchy. Perhaps if they had been prepared to co-operate rather than pursue their own interests, something might have been achieved. On the English side, however, though man-power was not lacking, the nobility were chronically short of ready cash, while over the Border the defeat of the Border Douglases by the Angus branch at the battle of Arkenholm, created a vacuum difficult to fill.

The Wars of Independence, by throwing Scotland into the arms of France, had created a situation in which that unhappy country was divided against itself; the French faction vying for power with those who regarded English influence as the lesser evil. Into this quarrel the Borderers entered with enthusiasm. The almost unbearable conditions under which they had been for so long compelled to exist had at least provided them with a natural training in the arts of war, and this was an opportunity to cash in on what they had learnt.

If it was Edward I who lit a fire in the Borders, it was Henry VIII, a couple of centuries later, who fanned the flames; and this he did by subsidizing the 'English party' and anyone else prepared to stir up trouble. There was a double advantage to be gained by setting one faction against the other. In the first place, the resulting turmoil in the Borders was likely to distract the attention of the Scots from attacking England while Henry pursued his ambitions abroad: in the second it gave him an excuse, should he ever need it, to interfere in the affairs of Scotland in order, ostensibly, to restore peace.

The Douglases, while they were still a power in the Borders, had shown no aversion to accepting English gold, and now it was the turn of lesser men to share in the bonanza, while their opposite numbers on the English side continued their raiding, secure in the knowledge that what was profitable to themselves was also a patriotic duty.

However, it was not always in Henry's interest to harry the Scots, and during the uneasy peace that succeeded the battle of Flodden in 1513 he became increasingly anxious to call off the dogs of war. In full cry, however, the dogs refused to listen. He and his predecessors had sown the dragons' teeth and there had sprung up a race of men who had virtually forgotten the arts of peace. For hundreds of years the Borderers had been encouraged to rob, kill and burn until it had become almost second nature to do so. Now they were told that their activities, which had once been so popular in royal circles, were not only to be discouraged, but visited with the utmost rigours of the law. In the words of Kipling it was, "Oh, it's Tommy this and Tommy that, an' Tommy go away", whereas it had been so recently a case of "Thank you, Mr Atkins, when the band begins to play". As with the occasional commando after the Second World War, they discovered that skill in killing had almost overnight ceased to be a virtue and become a crime.

It was all very well for the Prince Bishop of Durham, whose

possessions included a good deal of what is now Northumberland, to hope for a little peace so that "the poor bodies may draw to the Border and win their hay and elding* against winter". It was quite another thing to achieve it, when every able-bodied man was armed and trained to fight. Eking out a precarious existence among pillaged crops and attenuated herds, once the wages which went with active service were withdrawn, what were they to do? And the answer, as the authorities found to their cost, was that they took to robbing other people of their cattle and belongings. Licensed plunder had turned to private theft, accompanied, where necessary, by violence.

As they turned their cattle out into the common pasture, the villagers quoted to each other the Border riddle, "If they come, they come not; if they come not, they come", meaning that if the reivers put in their customary appearance, the cattle would not return, but if the reivers did not come back, the cattle would.

The primary industry of the Borders was, of course, agriculture—but not the comparatively intensive agriculture of more fertile areas. Corn the Borderers usually grew in sufficient quantities to feed themselves, at any rate on the Scottish side where, on the whole, conditions were less rugged and the soil more fertile; but their main source of livelihood lay in the raising of cattle for food, as well as draught purposes, and of sheep, mainly for their wool. Both activities, while requiring little in the way of man-power, needed comparatively large areas of land if they were to support a family in any degree of comfort. The increase in the birthrate since the days of the Black Death, however, had led to a degree of overpopulation that two hundred years of warfare had hardly succeeded in abating.

In these days of rural depopulation, we have become accustomed to a state of affairs in which the towns get larger and larger, and the inhabitants of the countryside fewer and fewer. It is not easy, therefore, to visualize the Border valleys that are now embellished with only the occasional farmstead or hamlet, as they were in their heyday. When one considers, however, that in Tudor times the population of Redesdale, and no doubt of Tynedale, Liddesdale and Teviotdale as well, was more than three times what it was at the end of the eighteenth century, and that it has probably diminished even more rapidly

* Firewood.

since then, it is possible to appreciate the overcrowding that existed, not only by modern standards but even by those of the past.

This was largely the result of the ancient law of gavelkind that still obtained in Tynedale and Redesdale, if not elsewhere in the Borders; in other words the Old English custom of dividing an inheritance equally between a man's sons. The apparently endless sub-division of land led to farms becoming so small as to be completely uneconomic; providing neither a fair living for those who farmed them nor a reasonable amount of food to supply a growing population. Even at Berwick, where some of the land is very fertile indeed, the size of the town, together with the requirements of an inordinately large garrison, made necessary the import of grain from Yorkshire as well as butter and cheese from Suffolk.

A popular saying of the time was:

> The father to the bough
> And the son to the plough

In other words, the father's shortage of land led to his reiving for a living, and this resulted all too often in his ending his days on the hanging-tree, or gibbet, while the sons divided up his land once more, and the dread cycle of hunger, violence and death began all over again.

Nor was the farmer's life made any easier by Henry VIII's discovery that the cheapest and easiest way of keeping the political pot boiling was by encouraging the Border clans to fight each other. It was on the latter's express orders that the Earl of Northumberland promised "to let slip them of Tynedale and Redesdale for the annoyance of Scotland", and Lord Dacre instructed Sir William Percy to "make a raid at least once a week while the grass is on the ground". Seeing that the Scots invariably retaliated, it is difficult to imagine how the Borderers were expected to survive. In fact they did so in the only way that appeared open to them—at each other's expense.

Nobody and nothing on either side of the Border were safe from the reivers. In the morning a man might be rich in flocks and herds and, by evening, be without anything; not even a roof over his head. Oxen, milk cows, sheep, goats, pigs and 'insight'*, all were grist to the reivers' mill. Most desirable of

* Household belongings.

all were the horses which were not only essential to the exercise of their calling but to supplement oxen in working the land. Even where they were not stolen, never to return, it was not unknown for horses to disappear, only to be brought back in an exhausted condition, having spent the day, or days, on forced loan to cultivate another's fields by what was euphemistically known as 'private agreement'.

Nor did distance necessarily spell safety, the English penetrating far into Scotland and the Scots lifting cattle as far afield as Seghill and across the Tyne at Blaydon, while forays into Weardale and even into Westmorland were by no means unknown. Boldness was everything; reivers driving cattle back into Scotland "as if from a fair". Even Alnwick Castle, with all its immense strength, was not proof against the raiders' attentions for, in 1596, they surprised and captured the watch, broke open the stables and made off with horses and cattle.

It has long been the custom to write about the Border country in which the reivers lived and operated as being wild, lonely, romantic and so forth, as if it were all of one piece. It is not.

At the eastern end, for instance, the frontier for a number of miles is the River Tweed, on both sides of which lies some of the most fertile land in Britain. On the Scottish side this stretches northward towards the Lammermuirs, while to the south lie the fattening pastures and arable acres of the coastal plain of Northumberland. In neither case does the land rise to much more than 400 feet.

At its western end, the Border begins in the salt marshes of the Solway; then runs north-west through country that is dark and secret, much cut up by rivers and (in the time of the reivers) heavily wooded. It is in the lengthy middle section, from the River Irthing that separates Cumberland from Northumberland, eastwards along the Cheviots, that there lies the typical hill country of the Border. Even then, it presents a totally different aspect according to which side of the boundary line one stands. On the English side is a country of 'white' grass and heather rising to over two thousand feet; bleak, unsmiling, windy. Yet the Scottish slopes of these same Cheviots are a green land of rolling 'knowes' and little woods. When Howard Pease, one of Northumberland's many historians, stood on

Windygyle and looked down on the fair lands of Roxburghshire, the Coquetdale shepherd who had accompanied him to
the top, followed his gaze. "Scotland shows like a fine garden,"
he said.

Not all the Scottish side, however, would have met with the
shepherd's approval. The hills of Tweedsmuir, indeed, have
been called "a wilderness of loneliness and wet moss", a description which would have equally fitted Liddesdale.

These, then, are the varying types of country where the
reivers plied their trade, though most of it, admittedly, was
carried on in areas which shared certain common attributes.
This reiver country is a land of fell and moor, criss-crossed by
little burns and sykes that drain the quaking bogs of sphagnum
moss and cotton grass; of stony outcrop and jutting crag. Even
now you can walk (or preferably ride) over some parts of it for
mile after mile without catching sight of habitation or living
soul. In the middle of the Cheviot country, at the head of
Coquet and to the east of Carter Fell, lies a stretch of upland
so stark and empty that the Romans are alleged (without the
slightest evidence) to have christened it *Ad Fines*—the End of
the World.

The wilder parts of the Border boast the oozing, stinking peat
bogs that provided—and still provide—such a formidable
obstacle for men and horses, while even the moorland itself
is in many places so sodden that a horse's hooves will suck at
every pace it takes, and the night air is laden with the swampy
smell.

From the higher, and to some extent dryer, parts the views,
as might be expected, are magnificent; particularly when the
wind chases the clouds across the sky to cast their purple
shadows on the fells. It seems unlikely that the reivers paused
to admire all this, especially as they preferred to pursue their
nefarious trade in darkness. However, when they found themselves returning in daylight with their ill-gotten gains, they
were probably glad of the chance which the lie of the land
gave them to pick up their pursuers at long range, and adjust
their tactics accordingly.

Nowadays the other most obvious feature of the Cheviot
country is the incredible stillness, broken only by the sound of
ewes and lambs calling to each other; by the drumming of an

occasional snipe, and by the cries of whaup* and peewit†.
It was not for nothing, incidentally, that the very name of
the latter was to become anathema in the Borders, for when
the Covenanters, themselves as often as not descendants of the
reivers, came to seek refuge in this same countryside, they
were to be betrayed to their persecutors again and again by
the peewits rising shrieking into the air. Many a reiver making
homewards with the cattle he had lifted must likewise have
cursed these otherwise delightful birds.

When a foray was to be run from one country into the
other, it was over this countryside that the reivers generally
picked their way, for here there were no great fords to cross,
as there were with Tweed and Solway, and few inhabitants to
see which way they went. The height of the hills was little
deterrent, the burns easily crossed, and the peat bogs avoided
by the experienced men who led the foray on their clever little
nags.

It is also a countryside divided up by valleys which, beginning as mere 'hopes' on the edge of the watershed, run roughly
south-east into Northumberland, south-west into Cumberland
from the hills of Dumfries and Roxburgh, and either south to
join the Solway or north-east into the Tweed. All this may
seem odd to anyone whose impression of the Border line
is of a west-to-east boundary, but as a glance at the map
will show, it runs, in fact, diagonally and, if anything, north-
to-south.

To south-countrymen whose lot it was to serve as Border
officials in the English Marches, and to other 'inland men', the
harsh and barren nature of so much of the Border country
came as something of a shock, and not only because of the
terrain. They found the weather harsh as well, with its late
springs, its cold and wet. Lord Willoughby de Eresby, when he
was Warden of the East March, once wrote that "If I were
further from the tempestuousness of the Cheviot hills and were
once returned from this accursed country whence the sun is so
removed, I would not change my homeliest hermitage for the
highest palace of all." Even Lord Dacre, himself a north-
countryman, complained to his superiors that the weather was
"very contagious" and that his people of the West March were

* Curlew.
† Green Plover.

in grave danger from the floods. The historian Camden may well have had the rights of it when he opined that the hardiness of the Borderers came not only from the constant warfare to which they had been subjected, but from the cruel nature of the surroundings that "hardened their very carcasses".

CHAPTER TWO

The Border Hierarchy

Being of great clans and surnames, this encourages their
obstinacy.   Sir John Carey

The ancient gibe that Australians should be superior because
their ancestors were hand-picked by the best judges may well
have been inspired by a much earlier one that the history of
the great Scottish families of the Border is better authenticated
than most because it is so faithfully reproduced in Pitcairn's
Criminal Trials. Over and over again appear the names of
Border barons such as the Maxwells of Nithsdale, Homes of
Home and of Coldenknowes, Crichtons of Sanquhar and
Douglases of Cavers. These were men who enjoyed all the
feudal privileges, including the right of Pit and Gallows that
enabled them to drown in their murder-hole, or hang on their
private gibbet, those malefactors who came under their juris-
diction. Close behind them in the power game ran the Kers of
Cessford and Ferniehirst, the Johnstones and the Scotts of
Buccleuch.

Unfortunately the perennial weakness of the central government had led to a disastrous amount of decentralization.
One result of this was that the office of sheriff had become
hereditary to particular barons, who were thus able to double
their influence, as representing not only themselves but the
king. Whether this state of affairs had in fact been allowed to
develop by chance or by design, the effect was in many ways
calamitous, for whereas the original intention might have been
to increase the crown's ability to control the Borders, the effect
was precisely the reverse.

On the English side of the Border the position was rather
better for, although Percys, Nevilles and Dacres also exerted

vast influence in a countryside that was almost completely feudal, the crown had managed to maintain some kind of authority by employing sheriffs and other officers who were quite distinct from the nobility.

Next in authority to these potentates came the lairds, whose exact position in the hierarchy varied a good deal between Scotland and England and even between Cumberland and Northumberland. In Scotland, where the conditions under which they held their estates conferred on them many of the baronial privileges, including in some cases that of Pit and Gallows, the distinction seems to have been a fine one. There is nothing unusual, for instance, in the courtesy titles given to Armstrong of Mangerton and his sister in Sir Walter Scott's edition of the ballad, 'Jock o' the Side'.

> For Mangerton House Lady Downie has gane,
> Her coats she has kilted up to the knee;
> And down the water wi' speed she rins,
> While tears in spaits fa' fast frae her ee.
>
> Then up and spoke our gude auld lord—
> 'What news, what news, sister Downie, to me?'
> 'Bad news, bad news, my Lord Mangerton;
> Michael is killed, and they hae ta'en my son Johnie'.

In Northumberland much the same state of affairs seems to have obtained, with the lairds of Thirlwall being known as lords, or even barons, and the Whitfields as earls. In general, any Northumbrian occupying a decent-sized farm or tower would be known as a 'laird' and would certainly expect to be treated as such. "Numbers of these men," wrote Thomas Bewick, the great engraver, "were grossly ignorant and, in exact proportion to their ignorance, they were sure to be offensively proud."

In Cumberland and Westmorland, to make matters even more confusing, any owner of a manor was commonly known as a 'lord', while a 'laird' was the term usually, but not always, applied to the eldest son of a 'statesman', or yeoman farmer.

Both the Scottish lairds, and their counterparts in England, seem to have enjoyed a curious Jekyll and Hyde existence. At one moment they would assume the bearing of gentlemen whose position justified them in accepting official posts and, in the case of the Scots, appearing at court in all the finery they could command. At the next, their traditional duty to their clan, coupled with an eye to the main chance and the itch to quarrel, would involve them in freebooting expeditions during which they shared in all the robbery, cruelty and violence that such expeditions entailed.

United to each of the Border chieftains by bonds of kinship, as well as the requirement to provide military service in return for any lands they might hold, was his clan or 'surname'. It was not essential on either side of the Border that members of the surname should also be tenants of the chief, and very often the attachment had no connection with land. Indeed, where for reasons of geography or otherwise, a particular branch, or 'grayne', of a surname found itself without a recognized 'hedes-man',* as was sometimes the case with the Bells, Irwins and Moffats, it might pledge its allegiance to the chief of another. Some graynes might also act independently of the rest of the surname, but join with it in time of feud.

The surnames themselves or, in the case of the larger ones, the individual graynes, seem to have combined to a consider-able extent the 'solidarity' and inter-dependence of a trade union with the pride of a well-drilled regiment. This certainty that they were superior to any other surname presumably inspired the traditional quarrel between the Robsons of Tyne-dale and the Grahams of Esk. On one occasion the Robsons had lifted a number of sheep from their mortal enemies, only to find that the strangers had infected their own flock with scab. Accordingly they are reputed to have returned to the Graham country, caught and hanged seven of that surname and (pre-sumably being able to write) left a note on the bodies to the effect that "the neist tyme gentlemen cam to tak their schepe, they war no to be scabbit".

Just as descriptive, if better authenticated, is the official account given of the horse garrison at Berwick as "mutinous and insubordinate to their constables, who are little above their own rank. *Being of great clans and surnames*, this encourages their obstinacy".

James VI was another who found little to admire in the clan system in general and the chieftains in particular who, he wrote,

* Chieftain.

had "a feckless conceit of their greatness and power", forcing lesser men to support them in the field whether those men were their tenants or not, while backing them in return in any quarrel in which they might become involved.

Wisdom, indeed, from the Wisest Fool in Christendom who, in writing this, went to the very root of the matter. Without loyalty, there could be no unity, and without unity no strength, in circumstances where the weakest must inevitably go to the wall. The loyalty of the clansman, or 'clannit' man, was towards his hedesman, whose commands he was expected to obey during his lifetime and whose violent death, or that of his kinsmen, he was expected to avenge. In return, loyalty compelled the chief to protect the interests of the clannit man, to afford him food and shelter when necessary, and in turn, to avenge him if he were killed.

The operation of the clan system, with its rule of 'one for all and all for one', is just another instance of the vicious circle which plagued the Borders for so long, whereby the inability of the central governments, particularly that of Scotland, to exercise control, led to men joining together for mutual protection, while the strength that they thus achieved made the task of the crown that much more difficult.

The position was made even worse, in the eyes of authority, by the custom of 'manrent' that existed on the Scottish side, which enabled a surname to recruit 'honorary members'. Anyone, however important, who for some reason felt he was not powerful enough to look after himself or his followers, could enter into a Bond of Manrent with a chieftain, whereby he undertook to be his man, to be loyal to him and to assist him against all his enemies except, of course, the crown. In return he would expect to be provided for and protected as if he were a member of the surname.

It was in 1541 that Sir Thomas Wharton, when Deputy Warden of the West March, reported to the Privy Council that the Scottish warden, Lord Maxwell, "had blown out at the horn Scottishmen to the number of forty" and that the delinquents "did not only make a rode* and did spoil a number of horses

* Raid.

and other cattle within mine office but also did set on fire Jack
of Musgrave's house". The Scottish authorities, when confronted
with this report, denied all knowledge of anything so unseemly,
saying that no Scots had been blown out lately.

'Blowing out', or 'putting to the horn', was the ceremony by
which a man was outlawed so that he could not return in
safety to his surname. If, for instance, a Borderer who had
been involved in a raid, or committed a murder, was not to be
found, his chief might be required to offer himself as a
"surety* that parties would be satisfied". If no chief should
come forward, the accused would automatically become a
'broken man' and his life forfeit, not because of the crime that
he had committed but because no-one was prepared to go bail
for him. If he could not be 'clengit and hangit', in other words
caught and hanged, his 'breaking' would be signalized by
proclamation at the market crosses to the sound of a trumpet.
This system was just one indication of the way in which the
authorities made a virtue of necessity by keeping order, so far
as they could, through the system of surnames. Either a man
was 'clannit' and there was someone to take responsibility for
his actions, or else he was thus publicly named as no longer
belonging to any clan. A hedesman who happened to come
across a broken man was expected, according to Scottish law
at least, to arrest him or face the consequences.

No-one in the Borders took this threat very seriously until
they had to, and then it was often too late. By the middle of
the sixteenth century, for instance, great numbers of outlaws
were to be found walking the streets of Hawick without any
action being taken against them, till the Earl of Mar, who was
Regent at the time, appeared, surrounded the town and made
proclamation in the Market Place, reminding the populace that
it was death to 'recett' such a man. No less than fifty-three of
the best-known outlaws were rounded up. Six were sent to
Edinburgh to be strung up, eighteen were drowned on the spot
for "lack of trees and halters", and the rest imprisoned or
acquitted as the case might be. This seems to have proved an
effective, if temporary, deterrent.

On occasion a whole surname could be decimated by out-

* Hostage.

lawry. Thus, according to the Ballad of the Redeswire, among those present on the day of truce were—

> 'The Armestranges that aye hae been
> A hardie house, but not a hail'.

In other words they were a 'broken clan'.

Men who had been outlawed either passed over into the other kingdom, where they might reasonably expect sanctuary, or into what were known as the Debatable Lands, where they settled down as professional thieves whose only hope of survival lay in living off the country or, to be more precise, whichever country offered the best pickings. By far the largest and most important of these 'Bateable' or 'Threip' Lands, was the area around Canonbie and Longtown, where there was no natural boundary, and over which the two countries had quarrelled for so long that it came to be accepted as a kind of no-man's-land. In modern times it might have been designated a de-militarized zone; a description which would probably have made its far from de-militarized inhabitants laugh till they cried.

Bounded on the west by the Water of Sark, on the east by that lovely river, the Border Esk and by Liddel Water; on the north by Tarras Moss and on the south by the Esk Estuary, the whole area extended to no more than ten miles by three-and-a-half, but assumed a nuisance value out of all proportion to its geographical size.

Here gathered a motley assortment of broken men who were English or Scottish as they pleased, "delighting in all mischief, and most unnaturally and cruelly wasting and destroying, harrying and slaying, their own neighbours". Here, also, were the estates of many of the Grahams (ostensibly an English surname) and of a number of Armstrongs who had moved there (under pressure) from Liddesdale, and a few of the Bells.

It was a point of honour among the Borderers to express their disdain for authority, by whichever government it was exercised, by offering sanctuary to anyone on the run. At any given moment, therefore, reivers from Teviotdale, Liddesdale and elsewhere, were to be found in England, as well as in the Debatable Lands. Conversely the ranks of Scottish reivers were swelled by Fosters, Hetheringtons and Grahams from Cumberland, together with a choice selection from Tynedale and Redesdale; the Bishop of Durham complaining on one occasion about "Cessford and Buccleuch whose best followers are amongst the worst headsmen of these broken clans".

Various efforts were made to clean up the Debatable Lands; Wharton, for instance, proposing to the Scottish Warden that each should supply lists of the other's nationals who had gone to ground there, with a view to surrendering them and starting over again. It was all in vain, however, for the dismal swamps of the Solway estuary made the assertion of authority difficult, and so there continued to exist there a kind of hornets' nest whose occupants sallied forth at intervals to sting and annoy with fine impartiality the inhabitants of either kingdom. If Scotland pressed them unduly, they threatened to go over openly to the other side. If the English warden failed to pay them enough to keep Scotland in a ferment, they promised to reverse their allegiance, such as it was. In fact they played both sides happily against the middle.

In the end it was William, Lord Dacre, who had lately become warden, who lost patience first. Ill Will's Sandy, an Armstrong of more than ordinarily evil reputation, had for long enough been in the pay of England, but now complained that Lord Maxwell, the Scottish warden, was making life especially difficult for him and his grayne. The Grahams, who were ostensibly English—at any rate when it suited them—were also righteously indignant. All threatened, with more force than logic, to 'become Scotchmen' if something were not done about it.

Blackmail was bad enough in any circumstances, but when it came to putting the screw on the warden himself, it was altogether too much, and he approached the Scottish authorities with a view to putting a stop to this kind of thing once and for all. The Scots, in turn, thought it would be a fine thing if this festering sore could at last be healed. Accordingly, in 1551, a joint commission sat to consider the building of a march dyke "as was done on the West Border betwixt Reddenburn and the Fell". Four different lines which the proposed frontier might follow were discussed, and agreement was finally reached on an earthwork running from the Esk just below its junction with Liddel Water, to the Sark, which it was to follow until it reached the Solway.

Hardly anything now remains of the 'Scottish Dyke' with

its double ditch, although its line is marked by a wood in which its eastern termination is just discernible. Each end was originally marked by a square stone bearing the arms of Scotland on one side and of England on the other, and on its completion the Commissioners and the respective wardens breathed a sigh of relief to think of the peaceful times to come. It was a forlorn hope.

CHAPTER THREE

Wardens of the Marches

To keep the wild people of all three marches in order will require men of good estimation and nobility.

Thomas Howard, Duke of Norfolk

The Debatable Lands were, geographically speaking, the only blot on an otherwise tidy arrangement for administering the Border. It had early been agreed by Commissioners representing the two kingdoms that the frontier counties should be divided into three Marches on each side.

The East March of Scotland originally consisted of the town of Berwick (soon to change hands), of that fertile stretch of land known as the Merse (or March) of Berwick, and of country running up to the Lammermuir Hills—in other words, all the eastern part of Berwickshire. Concerned with that part of the Border line that runs from the sea to the Hanging Stone on Cheviot, it was largely dominated by the Home family, different branches of which operated from Home Castle, Coldenknowes, Wedderburn and other strongholds such as Fast Castle in its apparently impregnable position on the coast.

Opposite the Scottish East March lay its English equivalent, which included all the north-east part of Northumberland, as well as those parts of the Palatinate of Durham known as Norhamshire and Islandshire, which were of such importance to the Prince Bishop. The western boundary ran southwards from Cheviot, while the southern limit was the river Aln; Alnwick itself being usually excluded. Herons, Greys and Selbys provided its 'chiefest families', under the general influence of the Earls of Northumberland and (eventually) of the Governors of Berwick, "the strongest hold in all Britain".

The Scottish Middle March contained the rest of Berwickshire and the whole of Roxburghshire, and extended as far north as Peebles, a town that, due to its general inaccessibility from the south, seems to have remained mercifully free from English raids. Kelso, Hawick and Jedburgh, however, provided not only important centres, but attractive targets in time of war. Originally, this March included Liddesdale, but the inaccessibility of the valley eventually developed in its inhabitants a corporate feeling which, together with a corresponding independence of authority and a love of reiving, made them a menace second only to the outlaws of the Debatable Lands. Accordingly the district was taken out of the Middle March and administered separately.

The English Middle March, in turn, consisted of the remainder of Northumberland, together with such districts as Tynedale and Redesdale, which were originally 'regalities' unconnected with the county, and Bedlingtonshire which was part of the Palatinate. The March was administered from Alnwick and garrisons kept at Harbottle and Chipchase. Compared to the East March, it was less accessible to regular troops and artillery, which could not, of course, pass over the Cheviots, but easier of access by the reivers who, further east, might have found the fords of Tweed difficult to cross. Ogles, Fenwicks, Collingwoods and Widdringtons helped to provide some kind of defence against the Scots as also, on occasion, against the 'robber valleys' of Tynedale and Redesdale.

The Stewartries of Kirkcudbright and Annandale and the Sheriffdom of Dumfries made up the Scottish West March, an area dominated by the great family of Maxwell with its headquarters at Caerlaverock Castle, near Dumfries, and by the Johnstones at Lochwood and elsewhere. Although there were a number of fords over the Solway, these could easily prove impassable, and the easiest way into England from the West March, as from Liddesdale, was at the extreme eastern corner of the March or, as Sir Robert Bowes put it, "the foot of Kershope or Kershope bridge which is a common passage as well for the thieves of Tynedale, Bewcastle and Gilsland in England as for the thieves of Liddesdale in Scotland with the stolen goods from one realm to the other".

The thieves of Bewcastle and Gilsland, to whom Bowes referred, were inhabitants of the English West March, which covered not only Cumberland but Westmorland as well. For some time the Lords Dacre managed, as wardens and as great landowners, to exercise some control over the district but, as the sixteenth century wore on, their influence diminished.

Headquarters of the March were at Carlisle Castle, which still stands much as it did in Tudor times, and garrisons were kept at Bewcastle, Rockcliffe and Askerton. During the latter part of the reiving period the former needed constant repair, and at one time hardly a room remained "wherein a man may sit dry". Nevertheless, it continued in use, though now only the ruins of the massive keep remain to show where the royal fortress stood. Askerton, on the other hand, has been fittingly restored. Salkelds, Musgraves, Lowthers and Carletons filled most of the official positions, though the last mentioned, at least, would have been hard put to it on occasion to say whose side they were really on.

The government of the Marches was in the hands of the wardens who, though first heard of in 1318, may well have existed at an earlier date. To begin with, there was only one warden general on each side of the Border; most of the work being done by deputies. As time went on, however, there grew up a more sophisticated system whereby three wardens on each side ruled through a system which in England included deputy wardens, keepers, land sergeants and bailiffs. At first the wardens were concerned only with defence, but gradually they became responsible, in place of the sheriffs, for the capture of criminals, for watch and ward, and for ensuring that the Borderers followed the host and took part in the hue and cry. As the Duke of Norfolk warned Henry VIII, "to keep the wild people of all three marches in order will require men of good estimation and nobility".

The position of the English wardens has been likened to that of a King of Israel during the absence of Elijah, while their Scottish equivalents had, if anything, wider powers still. Wardens were in fact, for all practical purposes, viceroys of the Border area, who were expected to interpret and administer, with the absolute minimum of assistance from the central government, a kind of Martial Law. So long as everything went smoothly, the wardens were left very much to their own devices, perhaps too much so for their own liking, for they rarely seem to have had enough soldiery or supplies to satisfy them. The greatest, if not the only, crime that they could commit in the eyes of their sovereign was to embroil him (or her) in disputes with his neighbour when it did not suit him.

In theory, all offences against the ordinary laws of the land were dealt with in the justice courts, the wardens only trying offences against the special laws applying to the Border. In practice, however, a warden was all-powerful within his own area, exercising powers of life and death over his people. If he thought fit to 'justify'* anyone who was 'caught with the red hand', he did so and asked questions afterwards, for the conditions under which he worked did not allow of over much nicety in collecting evidence. It was rough justice indeed, but at least the reivers knew what to expect.

The rewards on which a warden on either side of the Border might reasonably count depended very much on his own efforts, or rather on the way in which he interpreted his mandate, for the salary alone was usually inconsiderable. In addition, however, to his remuneration, such as it was, a warden was allowed provisions and forage for his personal guard of horsemen, together with certain out-of-pocket expenses; and he was provided with an official residence. His officials and servants, however, he had to pay out of his own pocket; or rather, out of the perquisites that went with his position. It was these perquisites, of course, that apart from the power and the glory, and the profit that influence might bring, were what made the wardenship worth while, particularly if he was the possessor of local estates which enabled him the more readily to turn his advantages into cash.

If, for instance, a warden ordered, or made in person, an expedition in order to punish the thieves of either country, he claimed, at any rate in England, half the nolt,† sheep, horses or insight that were brought back. If he imposed an 'unlaw', or fine, he was entitled to a proportion of it; while his position also enabled him, on occasion, to draw a dividend from any unofficial foray at which he connived or winked an eye.

Whether he was a senior civil servant, as was for all practical purposes the case in England, or the hereditary holder of an important office as in Scotland, a warden had to be a man of many parts. Like the district officers who were later to play such an important part in the running of the British Empire,

* Execute.
† Cattle.

he must be administrator, soldier, politician, policeman and judge. His principal function, of course, was to keep order within his own wardenry, and to this end he was responsible for the apprehension of offenders against the laws he administered—a responsibility of which most wardens were noticeably jealous. On one occasion, for instance, Lord Eure, when Warden of the Middle March, persuaded Thomas Carleton, the Land Sergeant of Gilsland, to hand over to him one Christopher Bell, whom the latter had arrested. Thomas, Lord Scrope, to whom as Warden of the West March Carleton was responsible, was quite angry, as if to say 'My bird, I think'.

Another function of the wardens was the collection of intelligence on behalf of their government. When Sir John Forster was Warden of the English Middle March, for example, his spymaster was one Ballard, alias Fortescue, who directed his operations from the vicinity of Wark-on-Tweed, and employed in Scotland "little blue-cap lads that will tell me how the world goeth". The necessity to indite frequent and voluminous reports on foreign affairs, as well as Border matters, must sometimes have left a warden wondering whether, in practice, the pen was not really mightier than the sword.

Nor could an English warden expect very much backing from higher authority. He was much more likely to be criticized and hampered by a parsimonious government and to be continually forced to justify his actions than he was to earn any kind of praise, or even recognition, for his services. If, on the other hand, he became too officious in prosecuting wrong-doers, he might well earn, like his Scottish equivalent, the ill-will of those who were envious of his position or anxious to benefit themselves at his expense. Worse still, he might involve himself *and his family* in a 'deadly feud' which could continue indefinitely. For instance, William, Lord Dacre, when Warden of the English West March, became unwittingly involved in such a feud with the Maxwells simply because Lord Maxwell, his counterpart in Scotland, had handed over to him in the ordinary course of business one of his own surname who had killed an Englishman. A party of Maxwells retaliated by murdering Dacre's brother, "hewing him to pieces with their swords". On another occasion, Lord Wharton had to be transferred from the West March to a similar position in the Middle and East Marches, because he also had incurred the wrath of the Maxwells, this time for

hanging some of their surname who were serving as hostages.

If the English wardens did not receive as much support from
their government as they would have liked, their Scottish
counterparts were in even worse case. The reasons for this lay
partly in the lack of money that perennially bedevilled the
Scottish kings, but even more in the system they adopted. Having concentrated so much power in the hands of the Border
nobility, they seem to have been content to let the wardenships
alternate between its members, whom they then left to carry
out their task as best they might.

On the English side, until halfway through the sixteenth
century, the crown similarly relied on local magnates to fill
the wardens' posts. When Elizabeth came to the throne, she,
or her advisers, had different ideas. The evidence was all against
the Scottish system, and it is arguable indeed that the outstanding lawlessness of the West March and of Liddesdale was
the direct result of the hereditary principle. Hence Elizabeth's
determination not only to select her wardens for their efficiency
but to ensure that they were 'inland men', whose personal
interests would not be such as to interfere with those of the
state. There was, however, one notable exception that might
perhaps be considered to prove the rule. This was Sir John
Forster who, as the younger son of a family of no great distinction, could hardly have been appointed to the wardenship of
the Middle March by virtue of heredity. Being himself a Borderer, he nevertheless had the interests of his own surname
to consider, and his final fall from grace was largely due to the
extent to which he had feathered his own nest.

As early as 1249 it was realized in both countries that the
sporadic warfare in which they indulged was bringing about a
situation in the Borders in which looting and violence, even in
times of so-called peace, was becoming endemic. In a situation
like this, the ordinary laws of the land were totally inadequate,
for the number and nature of the crimes committed were such
that the normal processes of law were too cumbersome to cope
with them. In the end it became obvious that the only solution
lay in some kind of Martial Law which, while encouraging
summary justice, would also take into account the situation of
the persons who were to be subject to it. In other words, it

would be as impracticable as it was unjust to treat a people, who had been actively encouraged by the state to indulge in more or less constant warfare, in the same way as their luckier brethren who happened to live further from the battle area.

But assuming that each kingdom was able to cope in this way with its own nationals, and within its own frontiers, there remained the problem of dealing with inhabitants of the other, under conditions where harrying and robbing the national enemy had assumed the nature of a duty rather than a crime. The solution; namely to frame a code of laws which would be common to both countries, and allow for mutual transgression, seems now so obvious that one may be tempted to forget that it is only hindsight that makes it so. Where else in the world, and when, has such a solution been attempted?

Yet this is precisely what was done; commissioners from each country being appointed to meet and work out the details. Twelve knights from Scotland, including the sheriffs of Edinburgh and Berwick, met twelve from England, headed by the sheriff of Northumberland.

Together they hammered out the *Leges Marchiarum*, or Border Laws, which, in respect of all major offences, substituted for the normal processes of law a rapid and effective form of justice that survived in very much its original form until the Union of the crowns. This code of law, however, was supplemented as time went on, not only by agreed additions that were binding on both countries, but by 'local rules'. A Borderer, therefore, was subject to three or four different collections of laws and regulations, which might well have been confusing if, in fact, he had paid attention to any of them. He was still, in theory at any rate, required to observe the ordinary laws of his country so far as minor offences were concerned, and also the by-laws of his particular barony or 'liberty'. Overshadowing all, however, was this new collection of laws, the breaking of which constituted 'March Treason'.

The code consisted, to begin with, partly of written law and partly, in the phrase favoured by the Privy Council of Scotland, of "ancient and lovable customs", and it provided the rules of the complicated game that was played out by the wardens for a couple of centuries and more. Whether or not the Borderers regarded these laws as being as lovable as their masters might like to think, they ought to have realized that they were luckier

in many respects than their compatriots elsewhere, for the
commissioners had been quick to realize that they must temper
the wind to the shorn lamb by fixing less rigorous penalties
for a number of offences. It was not, for instance, until 1560
that slaughter was regarded as a capital offence, though it had
previously been laid down that all movable goods belonging
to the guilty party should be confiscated and handed to the
opposite warden for the benefit of the next of kin.

Wounding was punishable by the enforced compensation of
the victim, mutilation being rewarded by the addition of six
months' imprisonment. In the case of theft the victim must
also be compensated and, if the culprit could not be found, he
must be "forbidden by sound of trumpet from all places"—in
other words, outlawed.

A variety of laws on which the commissioners agreed over
the years dealt with the vexed question of 'recetting', a term
that covered both the harbouring of wanted persons and the
receiving of stolen goods. Among 'international' crimes this
was one of the most common; an innocent man sometimes
being placed in an impossible position by being forced, under
threat of pillage, to recett a criminal, and thereby to lay himself open to a charge of March Treason.

One of the special problems confronting the rulers of both
kingdoms arose from the natural tendency of those on either
side of the Border, other things being equal, to make common
cause against authority. In practice this meant that, if it happened to suit his book, a reiver would think nothing of enlisting
the help of friends or relations of the opposite nationality in
robbing his compatriots. Intermarriage, therefore, or any kind
of trysting between Scots and English were forbidden, though
as the two nationalities continually met at markets and elsewhere the rule seems only to have been invoked when it suited
a warden to do so.

For long enough it was customary for Borderers to pasture
their stock on the other side of the Border, the only limitation
being that they must bring them back before sunset. They could
also collect such timber as they might require. By 1522, however, wood had become so scarce that the commissioners
forbade its collection from the other side of the Border
altogether. Hunting and pasturing of stock still continued, but
provided so much opportunity for mischief that eventually any

crossing of the Border without safe-conduct, except in pursuit of one's own goods, was prohibited, and any stock found on the wrong side of the line was impounded and the owner compelled to redeem it by payment.

Perjury, fictitious complaints and false witness—all were visited by appropriate punishments. If, for example, anyone swore to a man's innocence, knowing him to be guilty, he was to be delivered to the opposite warden to be imprisoned for a year and a day, after which he must appear at the next day of truce and be branded on the cheek with a key or, if both wardens felt like it, suffer the death penalty. Better, one would think, to be executed out of hand without having first to spend a year in a foreign gaol.

Within the framework of the Border Laws common to both, each country made further regulations applicable to its own nationals. In England, for instance, aiding, accompanying or harbouring any Scotsman engaged in a foray was regarded as "high treason and felony", as was the supplying without licence of arms and various other commodities. The selling of horses to the Scots without permission was also forbidden; even that most respectable character, Sir Cuthbert Collingwood, being very nearly convicted of March Treason for a breach of this law. So strict were the authorities in this respect that if a Scot were granted a safe conduct, even to come to London on diplomatic business, a precise note was made of the markings of his horse, or horses, lest (one supposes) he were tempted to exchange them for the English variety.

The giving of hostages, better known in the Borders as 'pledges', was an important element in the administration of the Border Laws. It was, for instance, common practice for a warden to require a 'band' or bond, of good behaviour from a hedesman, or the principal members of a surname, and to require the surrender of pledges to ensure its fulfilment. Sometimes bands, or 'assurances', were accepted without the requirements for pledges as when, in 1535, the Earl of Northumberland, accompanied by the most important of the county gentry, travelled to Hexham in order to accept bands from the hedesmen of Tynedale, who promised faithfully to deliver for justice any future offenders against the law; or when in 1596 the Grahams were required to give a band of good behaviour.

If a warden were so simple-minded as to put his trust in such "scraps of paper", all well and good, but it would be a poor-spirited surname that regarded them as anything more than a joke.

Actually, a band signified, for all practical purposes, a mutual agreement or oath, and was not restricted to assurances either of good behaviour or of support against a common enemy. A 'murder band', for instance, was agreed by those concerned in the assassination of Mary, Queen of Scots', secretary, Rizzio, and another in that of Darnley.

However lightheartedly the arrangement might be entered into, it must have been no joke to be delivered up as a pledge, for Border history is full of instances where hostages were left to languish for year after year until the original commitment had been carried out, whether by the restoration of order, the payment of ransom or the delivery of alternative prisoners. It was by no means unknown for pledges to ignore the financial penalty they might incur, and to escape from their warders. If they happened to be outlaws, there was not much that the authorities could do about it except, perhaps, demand fresh pledges. In other cases it was usual to impound their movable goods and if, as often happened, these had been previously spirited away, to 'apprise their lands'.

On occasion, pledges might be exchanged between the two countries as evidence of good faith, as in 1597, when the state of the Borders had become so 'ticklie' that a fresh treaty between the two countries was found necessary. Accordingly, George Home of Wedderburn, the Warden of the East March, together with Lord Home and "six well affected gentlemen", were instructed to meet a commission, consisting of an equal number of English gentlemen, at the Ford of Norham. The lairds of Cessford, Ferniehirst and Buccleuch were also bidden to attend, in order to hand over pledges for the good behaviour of the Middle March and of Liddesdale. These were to be exchanged for pledges from the Middle March of England.

Right from the beginning of the operation, the Scots began to make difficulties. First Sir Robert Ker of Cessford, who was at feud with the Scotts, professed himself unwilling to hand over the hostages from East Teviotdale until their chief, Buccleuch, had produced his. Rather than do so, he said, he would surrender himself (though he showed no signs of doing so). On the day of the meeting, all the English pledges, except two, were handed over (another was supposed to have been wounded in a Scottish foray, and a second to be "dangerously ill"), but very few of the Scots. No-one at all came forth from Liddesdale except Archie Elliot, and six out of fourteen from West Teviotdale also failed to appear.

At a further meeting at the West Ford of Norham, Buccleuch surrendered himself in place of his absent pledges, but Cessford, who had brought his, once more refused to hand them over. Sir John Carey (then Marshal of Berwick), in a letter to Burghley, described what happened next, when one of Cessford's men, acting, Carey was sure, on his chief's instructions, "shot off a pistol and withal the same man that shot the pistol lay down along upon his horse ready to fall off and cried, 'Slain, slain'. Another cried 'Treason, treason', whereupon the fray began". This took the form of an exchange of shots across the Tweed, the English, by their own reckoning, firing some two hundred, and the Scots returning the fusilade with interest. Mercifully it was, by then, too dark for anyone to see very much, and a fracas which at one moment had promised to become serious finally fizzled out.

Not so the argument about Cessford's pledges. Three times, in all, he brought them forward: three times he refused to surrender them. It was hopeless, wrote Sir William Bowes, one of the English commissioners, to expect such a man to behave properly. Meanwhile Buccleuch languished in Berwick (though not, like lesser men, in Haddock's Hole) while the villain of the piece went free. Buccleuch was not slow to accuse Cessford of a lack of honour in a letter signed "Your brother in lawe Buclugh". The only result was an offensive reply signed "Yr br. in yr owne termes, Robt Kerre", to be answered in turn by a furious epistle from "Yr br. in na termes, Buclugh".

For months the wrangle with Cessford went on; the English commissioners demanding his pledges and the Scots, in the shape of Wedderburn and Lord Home, playing for time. Eventually Ker surrendered himself in their place, and was 'warded' with Sir Robert Carey*, much against the latter's wishes, for "Habby" Ker was not everyone's idea of a house guest. As Lord Eure put it, he was "ambitious, proud, bloody

* Sir John's brother.

in revenge, poor and easily framed to any purpose in court or country". In the event, however, the two men got on increasingly well together, and finally Carey was quite sorry to see the pledges produced and his prisoner depart.

The 'warding', or keeping under restraint, of pledges was normally carried out at a safe distance from the frontier, which explains the popularity of such places as St Andrews on the Scottish, and York on the English, side. Their acceptance was an unenviable and unpopular task, for if the hostages escaped, despite their distance from the front line, their warders had to face the government's wrath. In Scotland the ultimate responsibility fell on the sheriff, whom the Privy Council was wont to surcharge with the prisoner's value. Thus if a pledge happened to die in custody his warder hastened to produce the corpse.

The giving of 'assurances' was, strictly speaking, somewhat different from the signing of bands in that the givers were not necessarily guaranteeing their good behaviour, or even promising to join in some particular enterprise, so much as promising their general support. The best known instances of assurances in Border history are those concerned with the establishment and consequent payment by the Tudor monarchs of an 'English party' in Scotland. The number of Scotsmen prepared to co-operate was, on occasion, quite considerable, with Armstrongs, Elliots, Nixons, Bells, Johnstones and Maxwells entering into assurances which in 1547 affected more than seven thousand. Foremost among those who accepted an English subsidy designed to make life more difficult for their compatriots, and therefore for their own government, were the Elliots of Liddesdale.

If the lot of those whose task it was to look after the pledges was unenviable, that of the hostages themselves was even more so, for if they did not die of disease, as might well be the case in the dungeons of the day, they might languish there almost indefinitely. The pledges exchanged by the lairds of Buccleuch and Ferniehirst at Norham, for instance, were to spend several years in York Castle. As time went on, their gaolers' demands became more and more extortionate until so much of the prisoners' money was being spent on the food necessary to keep them alive that it began to look as if they would never be able to ransom themselves. Finally, and it is thought with the help of Ker of Cessford, they planned to escape. Old Sim Armstrong of Whithaugh and his companions managed to break through the wall of their cell and liberate the others, who then tried to force their way out of the castle. They were recaptured; Whithaugh breaking his leg in the attempt. Nevertheless, he and his companion, Will Elliot, succeeded on a subsequent occasion; Scrope explaining in a letter to Cecil that "One Geordie Sibson, a notorious thief, with three more with him, having disguised himself, went in unto them pretending to supply them with money, and so set them at liberty".

Suitable prisons and towers were in short supply, and often those that were available were in a poor state of repair, as at Hexham and Harbottle. Gaolers, moreover, even if they were not plain lackadaisical, tended as members of 'riding'* surnames, to have divided loyalties. All in all, therefore, the frequency of escapes, at any rate on the English side of the Border, is hardly to be wondered at.

It was in 1518 that Lord Dacre had managed to arrest "ten of the principal thieves among the highlandmen of Redesdale" and, in the faint hope of finding someone brave enough to testify against them, despatched the prisoners under guard to Rothbury, en route to Morpeth prison. In view of the general feeling in official circles that he had not been over-anxious in the past to bring such people to justice, Dacre took the precaution of giving them an escort of no less than eighty men, and his own tenants at that. He then sent for the gaoler of Morpeth prison, together with the bailiff of the shire, to take the prisoners into custody. He reckoned, however, without his hosts, for the men of Redesdale, whose spies had told them exactly what was happening, crossed the moors to Simonside and overtook the party in Rothbury Forest. Here they ambushed the bailiff, killing him and six of his men; took the gaoler and four others prisoner, and disappeared over the moors with the prisoners, to seek refuge in Scotland. On a subsequent occasion the prisoners, from Tynedale this time, reached Morpeth gaol successfully, only for their compatriots to attack the place and rescue Cokes Charlton, "the most notable thief in that country".

It was only three years after the escape of the Redesdale

* Given to reiving.

men that it became the turn of Hexham gaol* to feel the weight
of an attack by reivers. Knowing that the 'broken men' of
Tynedale were particularly active, the authorities had given
instructions for special precautions to be taken for the guarding
of prisoners. One night, however, a number of the guards, aptly
described as "simple, poor men without harness or good
weapons", relinquished their posts; "some of them for to see
their cattle in their closes", leaving only a few on duty. It was
at midnight, when the simple, poor men seem to have thought
escape was less likely, that a large force of reivers found a way
into the prison, beat up what guards were left, and then robbed
them for good measure. Among the prisoners released were
Clem Armstrong, a couple of Dodds from Tynedale, and that
notorious villain Jerry Charlton, nicknamed Topping, from his
tuft of hair. He it was who endured a further spell of imprisonment, this time in Warkworth Castle, where the plague was
so rampant that he was almost the only survivor.

This was, in fact, one of the many occasions when the
inhabitants of Liddesdale united with those of North Tyne in
order to make mischief. A court of enquiry showed that the
prison had one iron and two wooden doors, but that the former
had inadequate locks while the latter had none at all. The
prisoners had not been fettered, but could come and go as they
pleased; their friends being able to come and talk with
them at the outer door, as in the case of village lock-ups in
some countries to this day.

Those in charge of Carlisle Castle seem to have been little
more careful in guarding their prisoners than at Hexham. In
1528 Richie Graham, who was thought (wrongly) to have
betrayed Dacre's plans to burn the Debatable Lands, found himself an enforced guest in the castle, but allowed to roam about at
will. It was not difficult to get a message to his brethren, and he
was able to "leap out by the privy postern which stood open
to the fields, where there was a man and a led horse waiting
for him".

A dozen years or so had passed when Sir Thomas Wharton,
as Warden of the West March, agreed with James V to exchange
one Andrew Bell, then languishing in Carlisle Castle, for a
number of Englishmen in Scottish hands. When all the prepara-
tions for the ceremony had been completed, he was much

* Now the Manor Office.

(*above*) "A stone that was once, no doubt, part of a prehistoric circle, but now known as the Lochmaben stone." (*below*) Bewcastle, where the garrison could hardly find a room "wherein a man may sit dry".

(*above*) "The Scots rode on into Redesdale and lifted three hundred cattle." The view from the Redeswire. (*below*) "It became the turn of Hexham gaol to feel the weight of an attack by reivers"

embarrassed to find that he could not keep his part of the bargain as the bird had flown. The prisoner was finally run to earth, sheltering with his own surname on the other side of the Border, and Wharton had to swallow his pride and ask Lord Maxwell, the Scottish Warden, to return him so that he could then be ceremonially delivered back again. Thomas Cromwell demanded an explanation. Apparently "the traitor Bell", having made his submission, had been given his liberty within the castle. Professing an unexpected interest in religion. he had prevailed on the captain of the castle on a number of occasions to take him to church, and had subsequently been treated with considerable leniency. When the captain was ordered to deliver him up, and sent one of his servants to put him in irons, Bell pretended to be ill, and persuaded the porter to put him up in his lodge until he was better. After a couple of days the chance for which he had been waiting presented itself. His gaoler went off to supper, leaving the lodge door open; Andrew jumped over the wall and the deed was done.

The aftermath to all this must have delighted the reiving fraternity even more than the original escape. Cromwell was furious at being made to look so foolish, and accused Wharton of not taking adequate precautions. Wharton, in turn, blamed the captain of the castle, who flew into a huff and refused the next prisoner entrusted to him, on the ground that no proper prison was available. Wharton then retaliated by himself assuming the captaincy. Nevertheless, escapes from Carlisle continued to take place with unfortunate regularity till 1605, when no less than 29 out of 33 condemned prisoners including, as usual, a number of Grahams and Armstrongs, broke out; followed a few months later by five more "notable thieves". In the latter case the gaoler's servants, having apparently learnt nothing from the experiences of the past, left the door open when bringing the men their supper. It was remarked rather pointedly that this was the third time this kind of thing had happened since the present sheriff took office; the inference, of course, being that the ties of blood and marriage had, as so often in the Borders, muffled the call of duty.

Carlisle, however, seems for long enough to have avoided the ultimate indignity suffered by Henry Widdrington when Ker of Cessford, accompanied by a party of twenty, broke into his tower at Swinburne and not only released the prisoner he had come for but took captive some of the gentlemen present as well. "And so, sounding his trumpet upon the top of the house when he had taken his pleasure, went his way".

One of the famous escapes of Border history was that of Jock o' the Side from Newcastle. The story really begins with the Lisle family, previously lords of Redesdale but then holding estates near Felton. The head of the family was that stormy petrel, Sir William Lisle, who had inherited all the violent tendencies of his father, Sir Humphrey, and added a few of his own. No-one ever doubted his courage, and his exploits against the Scots had once led to his appointment as Deputy Captain of Norham Castle. By 1527, however, he seems to have relinquished the post, probably at the King's suggestion, and it was in this year that he got into trouble with the Sheriff of Northumberland, Roger Heron. The latter, as was his duty, had charged Lisle with disobeying some command emanating from Cardinal Wolsey. Lisle retorted smartly that "having already ruffled with the Warden" he was quite prepared to pull the Cardinal's nose. For this, or some other of his various misdeeds, he found himself imprisoned in Newcastle, in company with his son Humphrey.

Also imprisoned in the town were "divers thieves of Scotland and traitors of Tynedale", which included in their number a most interesting catch in the shape of John Armstrong of The Side, a tower in Liddesdale built just below the junction of the Hermitage Water with the Liddel, who had been captured on a raid into Northumberland. He it was of whom Maitland of Lethington wrote,

> He is weil kend,* John of the Syde
> A greater thief did never ride.
> He never tyris†
> For to brek byris‡

A nephew of Mangerton, chief of the Armstrongs, Jock must have been a young man at the time, for he was to figure in history again some forty years later when harbouring the

* Well known.
† Tires
‡ Break byres (cattle sheds).

Countess of Northumberland. On the present occasion his uncle vowed to rescue him, and accordingly an expedition set out from Liddesdale.

> The Laird's Jock ane, the Laird's Wat twa,
> O, Hobbie Noble thou ane maun be!
> Thy coat is blue, thou hast been true,
> Since England banished thee to me.

The Laird's Jock and the Laird's Wat, would be Mangerton's sons, but there is considerable doubt whether Hobbie Noble (an outlaw from Bewcastle) was really in the party.

There was no time to lose, for Jock might well be hanged without trial, so, disguised as cadgers*, the little band, according to the ballad, crossed the Tyne at Chollerford and made themselves a ladder from a tree they cut down. Then, with the aid of Lisle and his son, who had conveniently broken out of gaol, and despite the ladder proving—as seems usual in these escape stories—too short, they rescued the prisoner, still weighed down with "full fifteen stane o' Spanish iron", which meant, apparently, that he had to ride side-saddle.

> O, Jock, sae winsomely's ye ride,
> Wi' baith your feet upon ae side,
> Sae weil ye're harneist, and sae trig,
> In troth ye sit like ony bride.

When they arrived once more at Chollerford, the party found the Tyne in spate, and there was considerable discussion as to what they should do.

> Then out and spak the Laird's saft Wat,
> The greatest coward in the cumpanie;
> Now halt, now halt! We need na' try't;
> The day is come we a' maun die.

The Laird's Wat might well quail at the thought of braving the flood in company with a man still wearing all that weight of iron. He must have taken heart of grace, however, for they all reached Liddesdale safely and lived to fight another day.

So did the Lisles who now, having burnt their boats, became full members of the Armstrong gang that operated from Liddesdale, and started on a career of crime which was to continue until it had the authorities of both countries thirsting for their

* Itinerant merchants.

blood. Nor did they lose any time about it, for on their way back from liberating Jock o' the Side, they raided Sir William Ellerker's park at Widdrington, and drove off twenty horses. The Council of the North retaliated by directing the deputy warden to burn a number of houses on Lisle's estate at Felton; to carry off corn, hay and victuals which might otherwise have proved useful to him, and to send to gaol various women suspected of spying on his behalf. They then asked King James to deliver up the fugitives, Lisles and Armstrongs alike. The king was anxious to oblige, but could not lay hands on them. Meanwhile the gang once more raided Sir William Ellerker (who had originally had a hand in imprisoning the Lisles), this time at his estate at Humshaugh; after which they went to ground in Liddesdale.

On two further occasions the Lisles got their own back against the unfortunate Ellerker, and the amount of loot they amassed attracted to their private army such experts in the art of reiving as the Nixons of Bewcastle and a number of Elliots and Croziers from Liddesdale. So serious were their crimes that Henry VIII ordered the deputy warden to obtain reinforcements from the garrison at Berwick.

Eventually the Earl of Northumberland was able, in his capacity as warden general, to report that he had held a warden court at Alnwick, where he had beheaded nine men for March Treason and hanged five for felony. The number, he said, included certain associates of the Lisles and, in particular, "John Armstrong who brought the Armstrongs to Newcastle when they broke the gaol there"; in other words, the Laird's Jock.

Seeing that the game was apparently up, the gang now left the doubtful security of Liddesdale and Sir William, together with his son, John Ogle, Will Shafto and Thomas Fenwick, 'gentlemen', and a number of lesser men, threw themselves on the king's mercy, dressed in time-honoured fashion in their shirts, with halters round their necks.

The Earl had lately complained that the Lisles "from their little house at Felton, the which joineth upon all my parks that I have in Northumberland, hath been the destruction of all my game there ever at all times". Nevertheless he was disposed to be lenient. Wolsey, however, did not share his kindness of heart, and all except Humphrey, who turned king's evidence, were hanged, drawn and quartered, "and the heads and quarters of them that were so executed for high treason" were "caused to be set up upon the dungeon of the castle of New-castle and in sundry other eminent and open places most apparent to the view and sight of the people to the high con-sternation of all the true inhabitants of these parts, and extreme terror of all other similable offenders". Humphrey Lisle (though only fourteen at the time) might well have considered himself lucky, in view of his admission of a list of crimes so extensive and so frightful that it read "like the tale of a modern Sicilian bandit". In the course of his confession, Humphrey asserted that, when rescuing Jock o' the Side, he and his father had forced the keeper of the castle to surrender the keys, and that they had helped to free nine prisoners in all.

In the face of the determined efforts that the reivers' friends often made to release them, it became increasingly difficult to find enough prisons in either country that were strong enough to hold them; as witness the escape of Archie of Cawfield from the Tolbooth in Dumfries in circumstances which, according to the ballad, were almost identical to those in the story of Jock o' the Side. The result was that more and more prisoners, if they had not already taken leg-bail, were let out on parole.

For instance when John Aynsley, a Scotsman, was captured by William Swinburne of Capheaton, in Northumberland, an arrangement was made to save him from "the rigour of justice" by letting him go, once he had promised, with the consent of his sons, to be "faithful, true and just" to Thomas Swinburne of Capheaton and to bind his four sons as well as "Sir Thomas Aynsley, Englishman" and all of the same name in Scotland, under pain of "reproving and bauckling".* He was to appear before Thomas Swinburne, or his son William, at any time on eight days' warning being delivered at his house at Falla, and not depart again without leave.

If the lodging of prisoners presented a problem to the authori-ties, it must have proved a worse headache to the reivers themselves, for where were they to keep all the people they kidnapped? These might well run into scores, if not into hun-dreds, as on the occasion in 1586 when 500 Elliots and Armstrongs descended on the Redesdale village of Elsdon and made off not only with great numbers of livestock but 400 prisoners as well.

* See page 153.

The object of such kidnapping was, of course, the ransom money that could be extorted. The Armstrongs of Whithaugh, for instance, once rode a foray against Kirkhaugh in South Tynedale and were pursued by the indignant inhabitants. The Armstrongs, however, saw them coming; laid an ambush and captured the lot, adding insult to injury by extorting a ransom of £180. They were doubly lucky, not only on account of the size of their haul, when so often it might only amount to a few shillings, but because they were able to collect it on the spot.

In the event of a prisoner being released in order that he might collect a ransom, the Border code demanded that he honour his commitment and, although as much as three months might elapse before payment was finally made, it was rare indeed that it was not forthcoming.

CHAPTER FOUR

Days of Truce

Yett was our meeting meek eneugh,
Begun wi' merriement and mowes,
And at the brae, aboon the heugh,
The Clark sate down to call the rowes.

Ballad of the Redeswire (Traditional)

Most of the crimes committed within a particular March would be tried in the warden's own courts, but this only applied, of course, where the malefactor could be arrested within the warden's personal jurisdiction. Obviously it was one thing to bring to justice those inside one's own country and quite another to go and arrest them in another. Even when the use of a safe-conduct, or of the right to 'follow a man's goods',* made such an expedition practicable, there would remain the difficulty of exacting compensation from 'foreigners'.

The solution, as agreed by the commissioners, was for meetings to be held at regular intervals between a warden and his opposite number, when each could produce the criminals wanted by the other, and reparation could be made. It was laid down, in fact, in the Border Laws that such meetings should be held once in every month; but in practice they seem to have taken place whenever it happened to be most convenient to the wardens concerned, which might not, in some cases, be until a considerable number of cases had accumulated. It was not unknown for a warden to 'shoot' a meeting, once arranged, by failing to turn up. More often it was a case of one principal having tactical, or even personal, reasons for postponing a meeting. Sir John Forster, that crafty old Borderer, was a past master at using this ploy to serve his own ends, but it was

* Cattle.

the Scottish wardens who seem to have been the most frequent offenders. So skilled in these tactics was the Earl of Angus (usually referred to in England for some inscrutable reason as the Earl of Anguish), that Wolsey was once constrained to lodge an official complaint. Angus answered virtuously that he had been so busy labouring day and night on behalf of his sovereign, and in defending his person, that it was quite unreasonable to expect him to concern himself with such matters.

In 1580 the delaying tactics employed by Ker of Cessford reached such a pitch that the English government was once again moved to complain, and King James ordered Cessford in no uncertain terms to arrange whatever meetings might prove necessary. Three years later, matters had improved so little, and disorder in the Borders had increased so alarmingly, that Burghley was forced to draw the attention of the Scottish king to the fact that neither Scrope in the West, nor Forster in the Middle March, had been able to persuade their opposite number to meet them. James promised speedy justice and "good contentment" in future.

It was originally laid down that wardens' meetings were "not to be held on the very March, for all men, ill or good, have access in armour, and such number of deadly feuds standing, it is hard to eschew brawling and bloodshed. Each warden, therefore, to meet his turn with the other, certain miles within his charge, at a town if possible, with not more than 100 men, under special assurance of the other officer".

In early days these instructions were no doubt properly observed but, as time went on, the holding of meetings near such towns as Jedburgh, Kelso, Dumfries, Alnwick and Carlisle grew to be the exception rather than the rule, and it became customary to meet within a few yards of the frontier, and in open country. Nor was much attention paid to the commissioners' sage instruction that no more than a hundred men should accompany a warden. On one occasion the English contingent numbered three hundred, while the Scottish ran into four figures.

An important stipulation regarding Border Meetings was that they were to be associated with a day of truce. From sunrise of the meeting day till sunrise of the next, a much-needed armistice was to be declared, and every man attending was considered to have safe-conduct.

Before the published day of the meeting, it was necessary for each warden to ensure the appearance at the designated time and place, not only of the inhabitants of the opposite march that he had captured and was due to hand over for trial, but also all those in his own march against whom complaints had been made by the other side. Bills of complaint had to be enrolled before a specified date, and it was these bills, whether they were concerned with murder, kidnapping, wounding, robbery, arson, 'recetting' or whatever, that provided the main business of the day. The bills were set out in a traditional form by the warden clerks and it is perhaps worth looking for a moment at a couple of those that were advanced one day in 1596.

In a field about a mile east of the point at which the Water of Sark flows into the Solway, and some three hundred yards from the water's edge, stands a stone that was once, no doubt, part of a prehistoric circle but is now known as the Lochmaben stone. It was at a Border meeting held here that David Graham of Bankhead, for instance, accused Sir Walter Scott, Laird of Buccleuch, with his trumpeter and 500 men, of coming to the "stone house" at Bankhead on the Esk, forcibly bursting and burning the door and "iron yeat",* taking prisoner Robert Graham of the Lake and two others and stealing a brown gelding worth £20 and household stuff worth £400 sterling. Richard and William Armstrong, the Queen's tenants in Gilsland, accused Watt of Harden, young Whithaugh, John and Gibb Elliot and others of "running a day foray" with 400 men, "arrayed in a most warlike manner", taking 300 kye and oxen, twenty horses and other animals and burning twenty houses, "taking and burning gold money, apparel etc. worth £400 and mutilating some of them".

Considering the number of bills that might be presented at a single meeting—at Bells Kirk on one occasion there were fifty presented on the English side alone—the chances of completing the business in a single day were probably small, even allowing for the fact that the officials must normally have worked with the speed of light. In fact, a second day had sometimes to be appointed. If, after the rough justice awarded him, the accused was held to be innocent, the bill against him was 'cleaned' by

* Gate.

the insertion of the word 'clean' or 'clear'. If he was guilty, it was 'filed' by having 'foul' written on it or, if the accused failed to appear, 'foul conditionally'.

The verdict might be reached in one of a number of different ways. The first was by 'avowal', where someone could be found of sufficient repute in the eyes of both sides for his word to be taken as to the accused's innocence or guilt. The difficulty, of course, was to find an avower who was acceptable; the Scots at one time flatly refusing to take any Englishman's word unless supported by a Scot. The second course was by the ancient method of compurgation—then obsolete elsewhere except in Church matters—which involved a communal oath by three uninvolved persons. The third was on the word of the warden who must "speire, fyle, and deliver upon his honour", in other words give his assurance that he had made proper enquiry and judged the accused to be guilty or innocent as the case might be. If, however, relations happened to be strained, as they often were, the opposite warden might refuse to agree to this method, which in any case was liable to backfire, for if a warden failed to provide within fifteen days the necessary proof of the man's innocence that he had protested, he himself became responsible for the compensation involved.

A fourth method, that of inquest of assize, was almost as difficult to arrange satisfactorily, for it entailed the Scottish warden choosing six Englishmen, and the English warden six Scots, to make up a jury. The trouble, of course, was that the Scots would recommend relations and friends living on the English side of the Border with which they were in cahoots, and the English would play the same game. It was by no means uncommon, in fact, for a jury, fearing reprisals, to give a knowingly false verdict; their excuse being that it was "better to trust God with one's soul than their neighbour with their gear".* As everyone knew everyone else's business, it would be quite obvious what was happening, and the objections raised against individual jurors would be such as to make the warden clerks' task impossible.

Assuming that a jury was finally picked, their first action would be to take the oath. "You shall clean no bills worthy to be fouled, you shall foul no bills worthy to be cleaned, but shall do which appeareth with truth, for the

* Belongings.

maintenance of the peace, and suppressing of attempts: so help you God." They would then have the bill of complaint put before them which, if they were to file it, would usually require the evidence of someone on the other side of the Border; a practice which, said Sir John Forster, led to a great deal of perjury. First, however, the aggrieved party must take his oath. "You shall leile* price make and truth say, what your goods were worth at the time of their taking to have been bought and sold in a market taken all at one time and that you know no other recovery but this; so help you God." It was for the jury to cut down the claim to whatever was realistic, aided, as they normally were, by an agreed scale of values.

A further oath, of course, was that required of the defendant. "You shall swear by heaven above you, hell beneath you, by your part of paradise, by all that God made in six days and seven nights, and by God himself, you are whart out† sackless‡ of art, part, way, writing, ridd§, kenning, having or recetting of any of the goods and cattels‖ named in this bill; so help you God."

The traditional meeting places seem to have had little in common except that they were near the frontier. A visit to the Lochmabenstone on the shores of Solway, or the meadows on the south bank of the Tweed known as Redden Burn or Hadden Stank provides a sharp contrast to the moorland ruins of Bells Kirk near Deadwater in North Tyne, or the mountain wastes of Windygyle and Gamelspath, where the ancient Clennel Street and the newer Roman Dere Street cross the Cheviots. Somewhere between these two extremes comes the flat (now divided by a railway embankment) where the Kershope Burn runs into Liddel Water, south of Newcastleton.

The whole business would begin with an interchange of letters between a warden and his opposite number; the tenor of which would depend to some extent on whether they were on good terms or not, and whether one of them had good reason for wanting to avoid or postpone meeting. Assuming, however, that a day was agreed on, proclamation would then

---

* Just, lawful.
† Clean.
‡ Guiltless.
§ Advice.
‖ Cattle.

be made of the day and place, together with a warning that truce must be observed and that any complaints should be presented to the warden clerk forthwith. In some cases that overburdened official might find it possible to get the matter settled out of hand, but in most it would be necessary to place it on the agenda for the meeting, meanwhile forwarding a copy to his opposite number.

In an era when the opportunities for recreation were few and far between, a day of truce must have presented to the Borderers many of the attractions of a bank holiday fair or agricultural show. No doubt, therefore, they looked forward to it with lively anticipation—all of them, that is, who had a comparatively clear conscience, or were not too actively engaged in the proceedings. As the great day dawned, the spectators converged from far and wide on the appointed spot, picking their way over the moors and fells and along the riverside tracks on their shaggy little horses and, as they rode, they must have wondered what the meeting would bring forth. Approaching the ground, they might catch sight of the two cavalcades, one from England, one from Scotland; the sun perhaps glinting on the armour of the wardens and their retinues and on the arms of the soldiers who were there to escort the prisoners.

On arrival, the onlookers would find the pedlars and 'tinklers' setting out their stalls; the badgers and cadgers* preparing to do business; in fact, all the fun of the fair. As they chattered to each other, old scores forgotten or temporarily laid aside, and old feuds officially taboo, the talk would be all about Gibb's Geordie's Francie and his chances of being cleared of thieving nolt on the plea that he had only been reclaiming his own, or whether Duke's Pykie's luck had run out at last. In circumstances where life was "poor, nasty, brutish and short", no-one would find anything unusual or macabre in laying odds that Will Charlton would be condemned to death.

They could gossip with acquaintances, and perhaps niffer† a little horseflesh; cast a wary eye at old enemies on the other side, and even make a rude gesture at them. They could buy fairings for their womenfolk, play at cards or dice, and inquire at intervals how any relations or friends were succeeding, or

* Both itinerant merchants.
† Bargain over.

otherwise. All would be in their Sunday best, and all armed, perhaps more from habit than any other reason, for they would not expect to use their arms except on rare occasions.

It is doubtful whether this carrying of weapons at a day of truce could have been stopped even if the authorities had wanted, for few Borderers would have felt fully dressed without them, so used were they to the danger that was part of their lives. A famous instance of the use of arms at a meeting arose at what has passed into history as the Raid of the Redeswire, which was never intended in the first place to be a raid at all.

It was on 7th July 1575 that the swire, or neck of land, where the turnpike now leaves the valley of the Rede and passes over the Carter Bar into Scotland, was the scene of a day of truce, the outcome of which is still celebrated annually at the 'Common Ridings' of Jedburgh. The Wardens of the Middle Marches who would normally have met there were William Ker of Ferniehirst and Sir John Forster. Ferniehirst, however, had not been available for some time, so he would be represented by his deputy, John Carmichael of that Ilk, a man who was soon, as Sir John, to make a great reputation for himself in the Borders but who, at a previous meeting, had been unable to get on with his opposite number, Sir George Heron. It had been agreed, therefore, that on this ocasion he would be confronted by the warden in person.

When the meeting began, there was no indication that anything untoward was in the wind. The two cavalcades approached each other and paused to allow the opening ceremony to begin; four or five gentlemen from the English side riding up to the Scottish deputy to ask that "assurance may be kept" until sunrise the following day, and the Scots returning the compliment. Sir Robert Bowes' explanation of this tradition was that "the Scots did always send their ambassadors first into England to seek for peace after a war", and therefore at other times it was only fair that the English should do the same. The actual site* on which the meeting would take place having been agreed, the two sides drew together to hear the proclamation reminding all concerned of the conditions of truce; the principals embraced each other and the proceedings began.

No doubt the wind blew fresh, as it usually does in those parts, even in July, but the onlookers would pay no more atten-

* Some 500 yards east of the present road.

tion to this than they would to one of the finest views in
Britain, that was there for the looking.

> Yett was our meeting meek eneugh,
> Begun wi' merriement and mowes*,
> And at the brae, aboon the heugh,
> The Clark sate down to call the rowes†.
> And some for kyne, and some for ewes,
> Called in for Dandie, Hob and Jock—
> We saw come marching ower the knows
> Five hundred Fenwicks in a flock.
>
> With jack‡ and speir, and bows all bent
> And warlike weapons at their will;
> Although we were na well content,
> Yet by my trouth we feared no ill.
> Some gae'd to drink, and some stude still
> And some to cards and dice them sped. . . .

The Scots, indeed, had no reason to think that any mischief
threatened just because the Fenwick's bows were strung, or
otherwise. All seems to have gone well until the assessors
reached a bill of complaint against a reiver known to history
by the unlikely name of Farnstein. In point of fact this was
no German mercenary, as one might suspect, but a young man
from North Tynedale in the shape of Harry Robson of the
Fawstone (now known as Falstone).

It was, of course, Forster's duty to produce Robson to answer
the charge against him, but it was not always possible on these
occasions to run the accused to earth: nor did it necessarily
suit a warden's book to do so. Carmichael, himself a notably
straightforward character, was always suspicious of others in
this respect. When he later became Warden of the West March,
for instance, he was constrained to write to the English Government behind their warden's back, complaining that "Mr
Lowther refuses me delivery of ane Musgrave called the Wood
Sword".

On this occasion, perhaps wisely from his own point of view,
but most unfortunately from nearly everyone else's, Robson
failed to answer to his name when it was called, and Forster

---

* Jests.
† Rolls.
‡ Protective jacket.

duly filed the bill for non-appearance. This did not satisfy Carmichael, however, who perhaps suspecting that this was just another of the ploys for which the English warden was notorious, demanded Robson's surrender. Forster promised faithfully to produce the accused at the next day of truce, but in vain, for the Scotsman refused point-blank to continue with the meeting. "No more can I make further delivery to you," he cried, "and it appears you cloak justice and are not willing that it should proceed." He may have added, as was later reported, that so long as Forster's own cattle were allowed to graze in the Borders undisturbed, he did not appear to be unduly bothered about how many fugitives, traitors and rebels went free. Afterwards Carmichael declared that if he had actually said this, it had been but a convivial jest and it is just possible, indeed, that he had shared one stirrup-cup too many with a man whose head was unusually strong.

Whatever his intent, however, the cap fitted so exactly that Forster lost his temper, and told Carmichael exactly what he thought of a deputy who made such remarks to his senior. He then poured oil on the flames by casting aspersions on the younger man's breeding. Carmichael answered with some spirit that he was capable of carrying out a warden's duties at least as effectively as Forster and, moreover, that he was just as well born.

All this seems, not unnaturally, to have annoyed the Scottish onlookers, who were heard to remark "Fye, fye, comparison, comparison". What happened next will always remain a mystery. According to the ballad, Forster—

> . . . raise and raxed* him where he stood
> And bade him match him with his marrows†,
> Then Tynedale heard them reason rude
> And they loot off a flight of arrows.

The Scottish version of the affair was that it was indeed the Tynedale men who, with a shout of "Tot it, Tynedale", took the opportunity of working off old scores by laying into the nearest Scotsmen, and thus starting a general fracas. Once the lid was off the pot, the wardens' efforts to put it on again proved about as efficacious as spitting in the wind, and soon the

* Stretched, stood up in his stirrups.
† Companions, equals.

Scots were being forced to retreat. It was then that the cry of
"A Jedworth, a Jedworth" was heard from the men of Jedburgh who, late for the meeting, were still panting up the hill;
and what might have been a rout turned into a pitched battle.
The Tynedale men, having lit the fire, were now, as always,
quick to take advantage of the flames; in this instance, by
plundering the wretched pedlars' stalls. Meanwhile the Scots
rode on into Redesdale and lifted three hundred cattle.

In the fight half-a-dozen Englishmen had been killed, including Sir George Heron, the deputy warden; and a number of
gentlemen had been taken prisoner.

> Sir Francis Russell ta'en was there
> And hurt as we hear men rehearse;
> Proud Wallinton was wounded sair
> Albeit he be a Fenwick fierce.
>
> But if ye wald a souldier search,
> Among them a' were ta'en that night
> Was nane sae wordie to put in verse
> As Collingwood that courteous knight.

Eventually Russell and Collingwood (Sir Cuthbert, that is),
together with Sir James Ogle, sundry Fenwicks and Forster
himself, found themselves in Edinburgh, much to the embar-
rassment of the Regent, Morton. Seeing that there was no war
between the two countries and no excuse for holding these
gentlemen prisoner, Morton returned them whence they came,
with a present of falcons. For this act of kindness—or diplomacy
—he was rewarded by his own people with the gibe that he
"had made a bad bargain for once in his life in giving live hawks
for a dead heron".

Nor was his action enough to prevent a post-mortem which
has lasted almost to this day. Were either or both of the wardens
drunk? Was there a private grudge between them? Did Tynedale really shoot first or was it the Jedburgh men who were
really at the bottom of the fracas? Whoever was initially at
fault, it was the English who came out of the affair worst, and
Elizabeth was not amused. Morton was asked to come to England to discuss the matter, but this he was unwilling to do and,
in the end, a meeting of the Border commissioners was arranged
at Berwick. The commission, however, could make little of the

(*above*) "Two thousand feet above sea-level, Windygyle is a wild and awe-inspiring place." (*right*) Carlisle Castle. The little oak postern through which Kinmont Willie escaped.

(*left*) Tarras Moss, "that large and great forest surrounded by bog and marsh." (*below*) "Among the chief conspirators was Richie of Brackenhill, a tower that still stands as one of a group of buildings on the banks of the River Lyne."

conflicting evidence and Carmichael, who had been surrendered to the English as an earnest of good faith, was released from York, where he had been warded.

The general opinion was that Carmichael, who was still a comparative stranger to the Borders and therefore unaccustomed to its ways, had come upon some of Forster's dubious activities. Forster, in turn, may have determined to get rid of the new broom by exposing him as an amateur incapable of keeping order. If so, it was a case of 'the biter bit' for Forster's own reputation was considerably tarnished by the affair. The Earl of Huntingdon, President of the Council of the North, accused Forster of general inefficiency, reporting that when he did so "Sir John did writhe like an eel". Killigrew, Elizabeth's envoy, who was at Berwick at the time, wrote that "the English warden was not so clean in this matter as he could wish" and went on to say, with some truth, "Peace or war hangs now by a twine thread". Happily, good sense on the part of Morton, and of Forster himself, prevailed, and the reverberations of the "unhappy accident", as the Scottish Privy Council termed it, were allowed to die down.

If, at a day of truce, neither goods nor cash was forthcoming, the next course was to find if the guilty party's hedesman was prepared to stand surety for him, or to provide someone else to do so, in the knowledge that if the money was not forthcoming within a year and a day, the surety's life could be forfeit. If (quite understandably) no-one was prepared to come forward, the warden must 'arrest' the wrongdoer by warning him to put in an appearance at the next day of truce. If the bill against him was then filed, the amount he was required to pay would not be the value of the sheep or whatever it was he had stolen: it would be increased by what was known as 'double and sawfie'. For long enough 'sawfie', however it might be spelt, was thought to have meant 'safety', or protection money.

The truth of the matter is that the value of the goods, say £100, was regarded as the principal, to which was added a 'double' in the shape of another £100, which was really a fine payable to the warden, and finally another £100 as 'sawfie', or salvage money to reimburse the authorities for the expense of collection. Subsequently two 'doubles', instead of one, were payable where the payment was in respect of wounding, and eventually in cases of robbery as well. The penalty for setting fire to a house which in the fourteenth century had been death (or ransom at the complainant's choice), was later reduced to payment of the principal with 'double and sawfie' and, in addition, six months' imprisonment. Later still, it was further increased by another 'double', and by the handing over to the monarch of what then remained of the guilty party's property.

Sir Robert Bowes was one of those who regarded the levying of only one double, and sawfie, as something of a farce. The valuations allowed by March Law in the case of animals, he said, were so ridiculously small as to leave the culprit, even after paying three times the amount, with money in his pocket.

Although the most dramatic part of a Border Meeting was the pronouncement of the death penalty, the most involved must have been the work that went on at the Assessors' table, for it was here that the claims for compensation between nationals of the two kingdoms were dealt with. It was obviously out of the question for each man whose bill had been filed to hand directly to his accuser the money he was required to pay. The only practical solution was a giant exercise in book-keeping, carried out by the warden clerks. Supposing that Will Armstrong of Liddesdale was held to owe Jock Hetherington £300, then that sum would be posted in the ledger to the credit of England and the debit of Scotland. If Jock Elliot was owed £200 by Lancie Robson of Tynedale, then the reverse procedure would be adopted, leaving a balance in favour of England after these two transactions, of £100. If the two sums had been equal, the process of justice as between the two countries, could, of course, be speeded up by cancelling them out. At the end of the day, however, there would almost certainly be a balance due from one kingdom to the other, which the warden of the debtor country would be responsible for handing over. Thus when the younger Scrope, as Warden of the English West March, did his sums in September 1593, they came out as follows:

	Sterling
West March of England versus Liddesdale	£3,250
Liddesdale versus West March of England	£8,000
So England has to answer for	£4,750

West March of England versus West March of
  Scotland   £6,470
West March of Scotland versus West March of
  England   £33,600
                                                                ———
So England has to answer for   £27,130
                                                                ———

Finally it was the duty of each warden to recover from the offending parties in his own wardenry the individual sums of money owing and, equally, to pay over to individual claimants what was due to them.

The payment of compensation, however, would be the lot of the lucky ones: those found guilty of capital charges would be taken away to be hanged or beheaded, as the case might be. In that case the offender would be urged to "have such faith in God's mercy as Dismas the thief and man-murderer had that hung at Christ's right hand"; this advice being accompanied by a wish that "your death may be an example to all parents to bring up their children in the fear of God and obedience to the Laws of this Realm".

The historic meeting at the Redeswire was by no means the only occasion when a day of truce developed into a riot, though such events were mercifully rare. It was exactly ten years later, in fact, that many of the same actors found themselves involved in a repeat performance. The scene on this occasion was Windygyle, in the Cheviots. Two thousand feet above sea-level, it is a wild and awe-inspiring place; enough, one would think, to dwarf most human passions. Here, near "Hexpethgate, called the Cocklaw", Ker of Ferniehirst was due to meet that indestructible old warrior, Sir John Forster.

With Forster came his son-in-law, Lord Francis Russell, son of that Earl of Bedford who had once served as Warden of the East March. The first intimation the authorities received that anything had gone wrong was a letter from Forster to Walsingham dated 28th July 1585. In this he reported that, at the previous day's meeting, "it chanced a sudden accident and tumult to arise among the rascals of Scotland and England about a little pickery* among themselves". Russell, he wrote, had

* Pilfering.

attended the meeting "for certain particular causes of his own", but against his father-in-law's advice, and "now rose and went aside from us, with his own men, and there being in talk with a gentleman, was suddenly shot with a gun and slain".*

As in the case of the affray at the Redeswire, some of the Scots had proceeded to take advantage of the subsequent hullabaloo to line their own pockets. They set on the Redesdale contingent, perhaps in order to settle old differences, and chased them four miles into England, returning with a number of prisoners as well as several horses, including that of Gabriel Hall of Otter-cops. According to this first report from Forster, however, he and the Scottish warden had succeeded in quieting the disturbance, and the latter had made proclamation that all horses and their "furniture" which could be found should be returned to their owners, and that gentlemen should be delivered as pledges "on both sides".

What must have been Walsingham's surprise to receive a further report from Forster, dated the very next day, telling a totally different story, but signed by thirty-two of the gentry who had been present at Windygyle, including (significantly) no less than four Collingwoods, a surname who had no cause to love their warden, or to support him in putting forward anything but the truth. This second report stated that, on arriving on Windygyle, certain gentlemen had been sent to meet the Scottish representatives at Hexpethgate, as was customary on these occasions, to "seek assurance that truce would be observed". Forster himself had then gone forward to meet the Scottish warden, only to find him attended by a great number "ranged in order of batell with ensigne, penselles,† fyfe and drommes, otherwise than ordinarye custome . . . in tyme of peace".

Without warning, the Scots had made a charge in which Russell had been killed, and had then pursued the Englishmen into their own country. Forster was confident that the fray had ben premeditated; an assertion which he repeated in a further letter dated 1st August. In this he also claimed that Ferniehirst had made no effort to stop the affair until it was too late and that "I laid hand on him and held him and caused him to tarry,

---

* The scene of the murder is thought to be where the track actually crosses the Border, and not at "Russell's cairn", which is probably prehistoric.
† Pennons.

otherwise it had cost me and all the rest that were with me our lives".

Subsequent events only served to strengthen the suspicion of foul play. According to another letter from Forster, Edward Charlton of Hesleyside had, some time before, intercepted the bearer of a number of letters from Ferniehirst, written in cipher, which Charlton had given to Russell who, in turn had forwarded them to the Lord President of the Council. Ferniehirst was known to have been furious about this, and Forster had advised Russell not to attend the day of truce. There is a certain amount of evidence that the Earl of Arran had been plotting a war against England and that he and Ferniehirst may have planned to revenge themselves on Russell for blowing the gaff, under cover of a carefully engineered disturbance.

The English warden subsequently dispatched a Mr Fenwick to meet the English ambassador at the Scottish court, and the latter reported that Ferniehirst had defended himself to the king, "with such false inventions as never was heard". The Scottish warden had then gone on to explain that the real cause of the fracas had been the stealing of a pair of spurs by an English boy named Wanless, whose family was "in grief with my Lord Russell for some particular matter".* Forster poured cold water on this explanation, for the quarrel, such as it was, had already been patched up by his own offer to hand over the boy to be hanged.

What has never been explained is why Forster completely changed his account of the fracas within hours of his first report, or rather why he ever made that report (and repeated the substance of it to his fellow warden, Scrope) in the first place. Was it the 'fog of war' which had so confused him at the time, or had he some reason for trying to whitewash his opposite number, which was subsequently overborne by the evidence of others or by his own better judgment? One thing is certain: that if Forster's change of mind had been connected with any obvious misdeed of his own, the Collingwoods would soon have uncovered the fact. Whatever the explanation, there is no doubt that the murder gave the English authorities an excellent opportunity to discredit their arch-enemy, Arran, and that they hastened to make the most of it.

---

* The Spanish Ambassador had it that the boy had bought the spurs from a pedlar and refused to pay for them.

CHAPTER FIVE

Kinmont Willie

And have they ta'en him, Kinmont Willie,
Against the truce of Border tide?

Ballad of Kinmont Willie (Traditional)

The fact that the Borderers' own code of honour did not extend to their dealings with officialdom in no way inhibited them from being gravely put out if officials, in turn, did not keep their word. Nowhere is this attitude made clearer than in the view they took of the inviolability of a day of truce and therefore of the proceedings which led up to the capture and subsequent escape from Carlisle Castle of that notable villain, Kinmont Willie.

Will Armstrong was born about 1530, a grandson of that Ill Will's Sandy who "with eight others of his sons, were pensioners to King Henry the Eighth who, for good service done, gave them Lands in Cumberland", but who himself continued to live in the Debatable Lands. His usual residence was at Woodhouselee, on the River Esk, where he was a tenant of Lord Maxwell. He was also hand-in-glove with the nearby Grahams, being himself married to Hutchen Graham's daughter, while his sister was married to another of them. Significantly, his own daughter became the wife of the notorious Thomas Carleton of Gilsland. His feet, therefore, like those of his grandfather, were firmly planted in both camps.

Kinmont seems to have begun where Ill Will's Sandy left off, gathering round him some of the best-known desperadoes of the Debatable Lands, who came to be known as 'Kinmont's bairns'. Together they ran forays deep into the English countryside, harassing both Northumberland and Cumberland almost at will. But it was not only England that suffered at the hands of Kinmont and his bairns. It was in 1585 that the Earl of Bothwell, Lord Home and Ker of Cessford joined in the attack on King James at Stirling, supported by the Armstrongs. "At this conflict," wrote Moysie, "there were only three or four slain on both sides but great booty was taken of horse and goods by William Armstrong of Kinmont and his followers." This was just the kind of battle that Kinmont enjoyed—a little fighting and a lot of plunder. It was not long, therefore, before he left the principals to pursue the royal troops while he and his "bairns' concentrated on the serious business of the day, carrying off "even the iron gratings from the windows".

By 1587 Kinmont and his sons were able to rely on the services of a fair-sized army and had, together with others, become such a nuisance on both sides of the Border that King James was forced to descend on Dumfries in order to make an example of them. Kinmont and his ally, Robert Maxwell, retired hastily to that inaccessible haunt of the Armstrongs, Tarras Moss.

Three years later, the Scottish officials had apparently forgiven Kinmont his misdeeds: not so Henry, Lord Scrope, the Warden of the English West March, now nearing the end of his term of office and, indeed, of his life. For long enough Kinmont had been a thorn in his flesh, but Scrope had never been able to find a solution to the problem he presented, a task that was not made any easier by the double dealing of his staff, and particularly the Carletons. Thus, whenever Scrope worked out a plan for circumventing his enemy, he could count on it being immediately betrayed and avoiding action taken.

By 1593 Thomas, Lord Scrope, who had now succeeded his father, had also begun to lose patience with Kinmont and his friends, who were again doing pretty well what they liked. They even ran a foray into Tynedale with no less than a thousand horsemen from Liddesdale, Annandale and Ewesdale, driving off three thousand cattle and sheep. On another occasion Thomas Carleton was despatched to waylay Kinmont and his merry men. Taking good care to miss them, he captured instead two well-known English reivers and then, to add insult to injury, allowed them also to escape, an operation in which he was ably assisted by the Captain of Bewcastle.

In desperation Scrope appealed directly to King James to "appoint an officer over against him to provide for quietness till the evil of the winter (that is to say, the raiding season) be past". James replied that he would seek assurances of good behaviour from Kinmont.

Scrope's direct approach to the King, however, did him more harm than good, for Sir Walter Scott of Buccleuch, who had lately been appointed Keeper of Liddesdale, where many of the Armstrongs lived, took violent exception to it. He and Scrope were two of a kind; both being young and ambitious, and both having reason to fancy themselves as soldiers. As a result, there was little love lost between them, and Buccleuch on this occasion took it as a personal insult that he had not only been by-passed in Scrope's dealings with the king but that doubt had thereby been cast on his efficiency.

When 1596 dawned, therefore, a clash of some kind had become almost inevitable. It was on 17th March that the two deputy wardens, Mr Scott for the Scottish West March and Mr Salkeld for the English, held a meeting at the Dayholme of Kershope—that is to say the holme, or flat ground by the Liddel Water, set aside for days of truce. It was a routine affair at which, as usual, "there was mutual truce taken and intimation by sound of trumpet and proclamation in their majesties' names to the troops on both sides before the meeting as the custom was".

Kinmont Willie was there, of course; easily recognizable, but secure in the knowledge that he could not be arrested. The meeting over, Willie trotted blithely homeward, chatting with the Scottish Deputy, Robert Scott.

Presently they parted, and Kinmont continued with three or four of his party towards his tower of Woodhouselee. On the English side of the river rode Salkeld with a retinue of two hundred, also going home. Shortly before the junction of Liddel and Esk the English seized their opportunity and, fording the river (probably at what is now known as Rowanburnfoot), succeeded, after a short struggle, in capturing their tormentor. He was then escorted to Carlisle "pinioned like a common malefactor, arms tied behind him, legs bound under his horse's belly". This, at any rate, is the Scottish version, of what happened. However, the explanation advanced by the Musgraves, who were in attendance on Salkeld, was that some outlaws had captured a certain Blacklock in a raid on Bewcastle; that they (the Musgraves) had pursued them to the house of Peter of the Harelaw, and had there discovered Kinmont Willie. The latter had tried to raise the country against them with shouts of "A Harelaw, a Harelaw", and in self-defence they had been forced to take him into custody and deliver him to Salkeld. No two accounts of an incident could vary more dramatically but, in view of what came after, there seems little doubt that the Scots had the rights of the matter.

Now the law regarding days of truce was, one would think, perfectly clear both in letter and in spirit. "Upon paine of death", it ran, "presentlie to be executed, all persones whatsoever that come to these meetings sould be saife fra any proceeding or present occasion, from the tyme of Meiting of the Wardens or their Deputies, till the next day at the sun rysing". The whole object of declaring a day of truce was to ensure that those who attended, and particularly the witnesses, could travel in peace without risking intimidation, assault or battery on the way. If, as Scrope was to argue, the period of truce ended at sunset, anyone with more than a short distance to ride home would run exactly the kind of risk that the law sought to prevent.

Not unnaturally, the seizure of Kinmont in defiance of virtually the only injunction to which they were prepared to pay any attention, shook the Borderers of both kingdoms considerably. Even if the skies had fallen, they could hardly have been more surprised—or more angry; the Scots because of what they considered an obvious injustice, the English because it apparently proved what Scrope's enemies had always claimed, that he was a perfidious upstart.

To Buccleuch the importance of the event lay not so much in its disregard for the inviolability of a truce as for what he claimed to be an infringement on his own powers. In a violent letter to Salkeld, however, it was the flagrant violation of Border law and custom on which he relied. But Salkeld "did excuse himself" and referred Buccleuch to the warden, who was taking his ease at his country house.

Scrope, in turn, replied that it was now too late to undo what was done and that even if it were possible, Kinmont was "such a malefactor" that he, personally, could make no move without Elizabeth's consent. Buccleuch, unwilling to bring King James into the matter, then tackled Robert Bowes, Elizabeth's ambassador at the Scottish court, "who, upon his desire and information, wrote furiously unto the Lord Scrope for the redress of the matter", but answer came there none.

Buccleuch had, in fact, come up against a bureaucratic stone wall. For years the English wardens had suffered at Kinmont's hands, and Scrope was not going to miss this opportunity of ending his torment once and for all. He kept Kinmont locked up in Carlisle Castle and proceeded to justify his own actions and those of his subordinates, protesting that "he pertains not to Buccleuch but dwells out of his office and was also taken beyond the limits of his charge".

Kinmont may not have 'pertained' to the Keeper of Liddesdale but he lived only just outside his jurisdiction, and there appears little doubt that he was arrested within it. It may well be that the warden was beginning to repent having yielded to temptation in holding on to Kinmont against all the rules, but it was now too late to draw back and all he could do was to try and save face.

The final excuse that Scrope made to his government, who were naturally perturbed at yet another threat to the peace between the two countries, was that Salkeld had been within his rights because a day of truce normally ended at sunset of the same day. Lord Eure, the Warden of the Middle March, when asked for his opinion, answered rather surprisingly that the period of truce was a matter to be agreed between the two wardens concerned, but usually extended from sunset to sunset! He confirmed, however, that if the truce was 'general' it would apply to all occupants of the Borders wherever they happened to be at the time. In retrospect, it seems astonishing that there could have been any doubt regarding the proper duration of a day of truce, or if there was, that it had not been threshed out long before.

There was nothing for it but for Buccleuch to take the law into his own hands—

> And have they ta'en him, Kinmont Willie,
> Against the truce of Border tide?
> And forgotten that the bold Buccleuch
> Is Keeper here on the Scottish side?

And have they ta'en him, Kinmont Willie,
Withouten either dread or fear?
And forgotten that the bold Buccleuch
Can back a steed or shake a spear?

O were there war between the lands,
As well I wot there is none,
I would slight* Carlisle castell high,
Though it were builded of marble stone.

I would set that castell in a low†
And sloken it with English blood.
There's never a man in Cumberland
Should ken where Carlisle castell stood.

Buccleuch's later defence before the Privy Council included two assertions that never seem to have been denied; namely that it was at his command that Kinmont had attended the day of truce and that it was "in his name, as Keeper of Liddesdale, the said day of truce was kept".

Kinmont's connections on the English side of the Border were such that there was no lack of spies in Carlisle, and these reported that the castle was 'surpriseable'. Afraid, therefore, that the prisoner might soon find himself listening to the neck verse on Harraby Hill‡ if he delayed much longer, Buccleuch planned a rescue by force; the final details being worked out at a horse-race at Langholm.

Naturally the Armstrongs were very much involved, but Scotts, Elliots and Grahams were anxious to take part. Buccleuch particularly asked that only younger sons should volunteer for such a hazardous adventure, but in the event his advice was ignored, and a number of seasoned campaigners appeared on the night. Besides Buccleuch there were no less than three Walter Scotts present, in the shape of Auld Wat o' Harden and the lairds of Goldielands and Todrigg. John Elliot of Copshaw and another Elliot (the Goodman of Gorrumberry) joined them; as, of course, did Mangerton as chief of the Armstrongs.

The night of 13th April was dark and rainy as a couple of

---

* Demolish.
† Flame.
‡ Standing on the gallows.

hundred stout-hearted reivers assembled at Morton, a tower belonging to Kinmont in the Debatable Lands, some ten miles from Carlisle. They were equipped with ladders and "instruments of iron for breaking through the walls and forcing the gates if need had been". The order of march was first a small vanguard, followed by a supporting body of about forty. "There was next them the ladders, carrying two and two upon a horse, and other horses carrying the instruments mentioned before." Following them came Buccleuch with the assault party, and finally a rearguard.

> And five and five, like a mason gang
> That carried the ladders lang and hie;
> And five and five, like broken men;
> And so they reached the Woodhouselee.

> 'Where are ye gaun, ye mason lads.
> Wi' a' your ladders, lang and hie?'
> 'We gang to harry a corbie's* nest,
> That wons† not far frae Woodhouselee.'

Dawn was only two hours away when the little army reached the River Eden "at the stony bank below Carlisle brig". The conditions could hardly have been more difficult, even if they eventually proved to be in the attackers' favour. Not only was the night pitch dark but the rain was coming down in torrents, and the river itself was shrouded in mist. Perhaps it was just as well that visibility was so bad, for the Eden was in flood and the sight of the channels on either side of the island that in those days divided the stream would have daunted the bravest.

It was the Scots' intention to land on the flat ground to the north of the castle known as the Sauceries Flat (now a public park). Taking their lives in their hands, they swam their horses, weighed down as they were with the impedimenta of the attack, across the foaming waters, and landed exactly where they had planned. They had reached the corbie's nest.

The raiders' friends in Carlisle, however, had miscalculated the length of the ladders necessary to reach the top of the castle wall. Luckily, further reconnaissance revealed the little oak

* Carrion crow.
† Lives, exists.

postern that is still to be seen to the west of the castle. This, Buccleuch thought, might provide an alternative way in if only the watch could be circumvented. In fact, this proved comparatively easy for, according to Scrope's report, "as it should seem by reason of the stormy night they were either on sleep or gotten under some covert to defend themselves from the violence of the weather".

Interposing a strong force between himself and any projected attack by the townspeople, Buccleuch detailed a couple of men to hack away enough stones to allow of the postern bolt being shot. Then, leaving a guard on the open door to cover his retreat, he and a couple of dozen of his men made hell-for-leather towards that part of the castle in which his spies had reported Kinmont to be lodged. (There seems to be no real evidence that he was kept in any kind of dungeon; still less that he was fettered). At the same time, the raiders made as much uproar as they could, in the hope that the garrison might overestimate their strength.

> 'Now sound out trumpets' quoth Buccleuch;
> 'Let's waken Lord Scroope right merilie!'
> Then loud the Warden's trumpet blew—
> 'O wha daur meddle wi' me'.

The rallying call that the keeper (for Buccleuch was never a warden) called for was "the old arrogant slogan of the Elliots", and it signalled the successful completion of an operation which, after the first setback, had gone like clockwork. Only a few of the sentries had made any effort to interfere, and they had been easily dispersed. Like Brer Rabbit, the rest of the garrison, together with Scrope and Salkeld, "lay low and said nuffin".

Perhaps it was the trumpets that finally inspired the garrison to take some action, for

> We scarce had won the Staneshaw bank
> When a' the Carlisle bells were rung,
> And a thousand men on horse and foot
> Cam wi' the keen Lord Scroope along.

However, one look at the rushing torrent of the Eden seems to have been enough for the pursuers, including the keen Lord

Scroope, and they agreed that discretion was the better part of valour. Said Scrope, alluding to Buccleuch,

> He is either himsel' a devil from hell,
> Or else his mother a witch maun be;
> I wadna' have ridden that wan water
> For a' the gowd in Christentie.

Instead, the warden ordered an immediate enquiry. He could hardly do less, for his enemies were openly sniggering at his discomfiture, while his superiors would undoubtedly want to know how it was that a royal fortress had been so easily breached. It was obvious that the rescue could never have taken place without collusion both outside and inside the castle, and suspicion inevitably fell on the Grahams, described by Scrope, when more than usually irritated by them, as "caterpillars" who gnawed away at their own countrymen, and as "a viperous generation" whose malignant humours he found himself unable to stomach.

In a letter to his deputy, Henry Leigh, he wrote that he was pretty sure that "the Grahams were privy and acted with Buccleuch in the enterprise of the castle—also the son of one of them brought Buccleuch's ring to Kinmont, before his loosing, for a token of his deliverance by him, and one of them was known to be in the castle court with Buccleuch". He might have added that it had been a female Graham who had discovered the chamber in the west wall where the prisoner was lodged.

It was Scrope, too, who first raised the cry that Thomas Carleton, suitably encouraged by the Lowthers, had also been involved. It would have been odd indeed if suspicion had not fallen on one or all of the Carletons, whose marriage connection with the Armstrongs was, of course, well known.

Scrope cast his net wide and further information soon came to hand, some of it in the shape of a couple of anonymous letters which named, among the chief conspirators, not only Thomas Carleton but Richie Graham of Brackenhill, a tower that still stands, as one of a group of buildings, on the banks of the River Lyne, a few miles east of Longtown. They also referred to Ebby's Sandy (Graham) as "the first that brake the hole and came in about Kinmont". Furthermore, Andrew Graham, when caught and interrogated, stated that he and two other Grahams had, on 7th April, met Thomas and Lancelot Carleton and Thomas Armstrong. The six of them then rode over to Archerbeck on the Scottish side, where they discussed the rescue plan with Gyp Elliot, Walter Scott of Harden and Buccleuch himself.

No doubt a judicious application of the 'pinniewinks* helped to elicit this information, and it may be thought that it was correspondingly suspect. Outstandingly so was a letter that Scrope assured Burghley (a year or so after the event) had been written by Buccleuch "to a great man in Scotland", but the motive for which, if it was genuine, is difficult to understand. Dated 12th June 1597, it began, "Whereas your Lordship desires by your letter to know of me what borderers of England were my greatest friends for the recovery of Kinmont . . ." and went on to name Francis Graham of Canonbie, his brother Langton, and Walter Graham of Netherby.

Whoever was, or was not, implicated, the immediate effect of the capture and rescue was to make the whole of the western Border more 'ticklie' than ever; Buccleuch and his merry men, according to Robert Birrel's diary, "puttand the said towne and countrie in sic and fray, that the lyk of sic ane wassaledge† was nevir done since the memorie of man, no in Wallace dayis". Quite apart from the 'wassaledge', the affair of Kinmont Willie was to have a most unfortunate effect on the relations between the wardens of the two countries. Hitherto they had, on the whole, acted together against the common enemy—the reivers. Now the wardens began to lose faith in each other's goodwill and to act on the principle of 'our country, right or wrong'.

Meanwhile, Scrope's reaction to criticism was to redouble his efforts to 'daunton' the reivers, making a number of official raids on them with the blessing of the Privy Council. On one occasion, however, he seems to have rather overstepped the bounds of what was considered fair and reasonable, and this resulted in the Scottish commissioners making an official complaint that he had led in person an army of two thousand men into Liddesdale where he had "burned 24 onsets of houses and carried off all the goods within 4 miles of bounds. They coupled the men their prisoners two and two together in leash like

* Thumbscrews.
† Turmoil.

dogs", while leaving sixty or eighty children "stripped of their clothes and sarks* . . . and exposed to the injury of wind and weather, whereby nine or ten infants perished within eight days thereafter". The English commissioners remained singularly unmoved, pointing out with some truth that the raid had been carried out "in the greatest heat of summer". "It is no novelty," they went on blandly, "but an ancient custom, for the English warden to assist his opposite and the Keeper of Liddesdale to ride on and harry such thieves and on occasion to do so at his own hand".

Scrope, however, did not allow his attacks on the Scots, who had liberated his captive, to interfere with his smelling out those in his own wardenry who had been involved, and eventually he brought the total of Graham hedesmen awaiting trial up to six. These he despatched to London in charge of a strong guard, to see what the Privy Council could make of them. There seemed little doubt of their complicity in the rescue, but neither the Queen nor Burghley was anxious to make matters any worse than they already were, and accordingly returned all six to Scrope to be bound over. On 24th September they arrived back in Carlisle "in great flaunt, and hunting by the way". There they dismounted in order to have dinner, and annoyed their escort a good deal by telling them, and anyone else who cared to listen, exactly what they thought of the warden. Only three months had elapsed, however, when the six found themselves and their followers so harried that they made submission to Scrope on their knees, presenting him with a petition in which, as earnest of their change of heart, they offered to take part in a hue and cry against certain Scots. The virtue of their submission must have been somewhat tarnished by the fact that it included "most impudent allegations against the county magistrates" who, said the Grahams, were anxious to cut their throats, if only they dared.

It was not long after Kinmont had returned to the bosom of his family that he was in trouble once again. Thomas Carleton, with a party of Grahams and sundry Scotsmen, had sacked Gilsland, and Scrope ordered a warden rode† to avenge the deed. Unable, however, to run the real culprits to earth, the posse descended instead upon the warden's arch-enemy and

* Shirts.
† Raid.

"Hermitage still presides over Liddesdale with a majesty largely unimpaired by its lack of a roof."

(*above*) "Carlenrig . . . the old churchyard where tradition has it that Johnny Armstrong and his men now lie at peace." (*below*) "John murdred was at Carlinrigg. . . ." [*sic.*]

TRADITION RECORDS
THAT NEAR THIS SPOT WERE BURIED
JOHN ARMSTRONG OF GILNOCKIE
AND
....

took three hundred of his cattle and horses with which to recompense the people of Gilsland. The Grahams, however, alerted to what was going on, ambushed the official party and made off with the lot.

Despite these afflictions, Kinmont's remained a name to conjure with; King James even going so far in his differences with the Kirk as to threaten its ministers with the possibility that he would call upon "Will Kinmond" and his "Southland men" to assist him. Next year we hear of him, with the gang of ruffians known as Sandie's Bairns, attending the Border race meetings and engaging in the forbidden practice of buying English horses to sell in Scotland, while in 1600 yet another raid on his house was excused by Sir Richard Lowther as retribution for horse-stealing.

Scrope was not one to give up, once he had set his hand to the plough—or, in this case, the harrow. Next year he organized yet another raid against Kinmont, but by this time King James had had enough of these apparently endless excursions into Scotland, on the plea of "pursuing English goods", but really, he suspected, in pursuance of a vendetta against the man whose rescue had so wounded Scrope's pride. He complained to "his Royal cousin", who asked the warden for an explanation. "I thought to do a favour, rather than deserve a complaint", Scrope answered pathetically.

Finally Kinmont died, though we do not know when, nor where he was buried. His name lives on, however, not only in ballad and fable but in history, too, as the unwilling proof that a day of truce could not be violated with impunity.

CHAPTER SIX

Warden Raids and Johnny Armstrong

And by my faith, the gate-ward said,
I think 'twill prove a Warden-Raid.
Sir Walter Scott, *The Lay of the Last Minstrel*

In time of war the wardens acted as independent commanders, carrying out quite extensive operations against the enemy, and it was only when a major campaign was ordered by the monarch that generals of national reputation took command. Between wars the position did not alter greatly, and expeditions conducted by a warden, whether English or Scottish, for political purposes still persisted. Of such a kind were the three raids into Teviotdale that Thomas, Lord Dacre, ordered soon after Flodden, when his brother Philip, with a thousand men, burnt Ruecastle, and Sir Roger Fenwick destroyed Lanton.

It was just after Flodden itself that the Abbot of Hexham and his men descended on Hawick, whose defenders, thanks to their losses in the battle, consisted mainly of old men and boys. It was a couple of hundred of the 'young callants' who, discovering that the English were encamped at the pool of Hornshole, some two miles from the town, surprised and routed them and captured their banner. Not only is this famous victory commemorated by a stone at the west end of the High Street but by the high spot of the annual Common Riding when the Cornet (chosen from the unmarried callants) rides with the replica of the abbot's banner.

Over the next few years the Scots, encouraged by English cruelties, made a number of forays. Henry VIII, his patience finally exhausted, ordered Sir William Eure "to let slip as many under his rule as should do the Scots three hurts for one".

And so the ghastly business of 'eye for eye, tooth for tooth' continued. In 1532 the Earl of Northumberland ravaged the Scottish Middle March once more, and Buccleuch, Cessford and Ferniehirst joined forces in order to retaliate. Next year, war broke out again, the English suffering defeat at Hadden Rigg, a disgrace which stirred Henry to further efforts, and the Scottish retaliation under Oliver Sinclair only led to an ignominious rout, when the English Borderers, pricking round the flanks of the Scottish army, 'weared'* them, like sheep, into Solway Moss.

Two years later came the infamous expedition headed by Sir Ralph Eure and Sir Brian Layton, when no less than 192 towers, bastles and churches were destroyed and untold plunder carried off. In view of these barbarities it must have been some consolation to the Scots that, lying in wait at Ancrum Moor, they managed to surprise and kill Eure and no less than eight hundred of the English, taking a thousand prisoners and (incredibly) losing only two of their own number.

1544 saw the equally outrageous expedition of the Earl of Hertford but, with the death of Henry VIII a couple of years later, expeditions on this sort of scale virtually ceased; notable exceptions being those of Hertford (now Duke of Somerset) in 1547, and of the Earl of Sussex in 1570.

A warden raid, in the accepted sense of the words, was something quite distinct from a campaign ordered by higher authority. There were three main reasons why a warden should feel it necessary to take such action. In the first place, it often proved difficult to bring to justice a reiver whose surname, in conformity with Border tradition, were determined to shelter him. In these circumstances enquiry was often unprofitable, and individual punishment impossible; so that it might be expedient for all to suffer for the sins of one. Alternatively, if the inhabitants of either country had recently run a foray, it was the warden's right to 'pursue the goods' of the complainant even if it should mean crossing the Border. Finally, the activities of a particular surname might become so obnoxious as to warrant the mounting of an expedition "accompanied by the entire force of the wardenry and with displayed banners" and the laying waste of the area, with fire and sword.

In an effort to restrain over-zealous wardens, the treaty of

* Rounded up.

1484 laid down that a 'Warden Rode', as it was universally known, must on no account be entered upon without leave from higher authority, on pain of the instigator being declared rebel and traitor. A strict interpretation of this law, however, was obviously quite unacceptable to an official whose only hope of success often lay in immediate pursuit; though a distinction might sometimes be drawn between recovery of goods, which would brook no delay, and retaliation which, by definition, was much less urgent.

Occasionally it was considered advisable to conduct an extended rode, which in Scotland would probably be led by the king in person, but in England by the warden, or someone on his behalf. An example of such an expedition is the lengthy visit that Thomas Carleton paid to Dumfriesshire during which he captured the Johnstone stronghold of Lochwood. So unpopular, however, were such 'bouties' with the levies who were legally bound to take part that eventually it was decreed, at any rate in England, that those assisting the warden should be allowed to return home after one day and a night.

It was some years after Carleton's rode that Lord Wharton ordered "his servant Hob's Robin" to "do a notable displeasure against the Laird Buccleuch", and went on to say that he should, "if it were possible, get some of his sheep in Ettrick Forest". The outcome was the burning of a 'town', the killing of two Scotsmen and the taking of two prisoners and no less than fourteen hundred sheep, a hundred of which "they did also give to a Scotsman that had his horse slain at the burning of the town".

Probably the longest lasting, and certainly the most thoroughly planned and best executed rode, was that of Sir Robert Carey into Liddesdale. The Armstrongs had recently made a large-scale attack on Haltwhistle, in which Sim of the Cathills had been shot by one of the Ridleys, and Carey, who had lately succeeded Lord Eure as Warden of the Middle March, was determined to put the fear of God into the inhabitants of that "valley of robbers". When he took office, he had been offered a hundred soldiers to form the nucleus of his warden's force, but had only accepted forty. These Carey took along with him, together with his deputies, Sir Henry Widdrington, and Sir William Fenwick, some fifty or sixty gentlemen who had volunteered for the expedition, and a hundred lesser men.

The Armstrongs, as was their custom when they had stirred up a hornet's nest, collected their families and their belongings, horses, cattle and sheep, and retired in good order to Tarras Moss, that "large and great forest . . . surrounded by bog and marsh" through which no-one but themselves knew the paths. There was enough dry ground within the Moss for themselves and their herds, and plenty of timber with which to build shelters. It was then the middle of June and they were quite content to stay there all summer.

From this safe retreat they sent sarcastic messages to Carey, saying that he had their permission to visit their country for as long as the weather would let him. He reminded them, the Armstrongs added, of the puff of a haggis; hot at first but soon to cool off. When winter arrived they would "play their parts and keep him waking".

Carey, however, was in no hurry, having made provision for just such an occurrence. "By the help of the foot of Redesdale and Tynedale," he wrote in his Memoirs, "we had soon built a pretty fort and, within it we had all cabins made to lie in and every one brought beds and mattresses to lie on." Carey was too experienced a soldier to disdain the art of making himself comfortable, and he was quite content to stay on the dry ground he had chosen, for as long as a couple of months if need be. Nor was he as simple as the Armstrongs seemed to think, for placing a watch on the English side of the Moss, he collected enough reinforcements to send 150 round to the other side where the going was easier. By this strategem he succeeded in bolting the Armstrongs from their burrow and, in the ensuing fray, carried on from both sides of the Moss, he managed to capture five of the most important of them as well as a number of sheep and cattle.

The Armstrongs had indeed lost face, and they were quick to put about a story, which may or may not have been true, to the effect that while Carey had been in Liddesdale *they* had been raiding *him*, and had sent him part of one of his own cows with the message that here was some English beef in case he might run short of rations.

It seems to have been generally accepted that a warden was justified in retaliating immediately against offenders from the other side of the Border. If the rode were disproportionately large, however, or particularly brutal, it might well cause resentment; the Scottish authorities complaining on one occasion that a posse sent out by Sir John Carey had killed and carved up one John Daglish, a Scottish thief. The warden was constrained, in answer to Burghley's enquiry, to write that it grieved him that there should be so much fuss made about killing "a notable thief". "And, my good Lord," he went on, "for your honour's better satisfaction, that it was not so barbarously nor butcherly done as you think it to be. It should seem your honour hath been wrongfully informed in saying he was cut in many pieces after his death—for if he had been cut in many pieces he could not a-lived till the next morning, as themselves reported he did—which shows he was not cut in very many pieces."

The younger Scrope made himself very unpopular by his constant attacks on Kinmont Willie, and it was not long afterwards that he was in trouble again when King James complained to the English government of "some gentlemen of his wardenry" despoiling the Scots. He had thought, wrote Scrope plaintively, that he would have earned the king's thanks, rather than his displeasure, for having captured the murderers of his warden (Carmichael). The rumble of displeasure still continued, however, and Scrope wrote again regarding the "heavy complaint against me for a little revenge I have taken on those thieves who never rest spoiling us. As yet [referring to King James] we have but a leetle tickled him about the edges". A month later he was still in correspondence over the matter, this time with Nicolson, the ambassador at the Scottish Court, when he referred indignantly to "those marmosets that incense that King with those false reports against me".

The forces at the wardens' disposal were of three kinds. In the first place, the law required every able-bodied man of the Border counties to bear arms and turn out when required, in order to repel invasion or to help the warden to keep order. For this purpose the most meticulous registers, or muster-rolls, were maintained in England, showing by 'towns' the numbers of men available, often by name, and whether they were just 'able'—that is to say, equipped as foot-soldiers—or 'able in horse and harness'.

Muster days were held periodically and, as the majority of the male population would be eligible for service, these amounted to public holidays. "There is never a plough going," remarked a contemporary writer, "in Norhamshire or Bamburghshire that day; it is their principal feast".

Not content with a general classification of those available for service, the muster-rolls in many cases noted the actual weapons in the possession of each man; which in fact varied somewhat from district to district. In a muster of the English East March in 1584, for instance, most were armed only with a spear, but a few with bows. A few years earlier, an enquiry into the number of able men in the West March had revealed that the majority of those living close to the Border, in addition to a steel cap and the protective jacket known as a jack, possessed spears; while those further south preferred bows or bills.* One unwilling hero is described as being ready with a pikestaff, and another with a pitchfork.

Perhaps the fullest list of arms and armour is to be found in a Scottish ordinance of 1540 which laid down that "unlanded gentlemen and yeomen have jacks of plate, halbriks, splents, sallat, or steel bonnet, with pisan, or gorget, and all to wear swords". These terms demand some explanation. The jack which, with a steel cap or bonnet (known sometimes as a knapscall or morion), provided the basic amount of armour in the Borders, has been described as a loose-fitting tunic reaching to mid-thigh; of many folds of cloth, stuffed, quilted and covered in reindeer hide; though no doubt cowhide would have made an acceptable substitute. This could be worn, if the greatest possible protection was required, over a hauberk or coat of mail. Splents were shoulder-pieces, or sleeves, of plate armour: a sallat was an infantry helmet with protection for the ears and neck; while a gorget provided protection for the throat.

A light horseman of the Borders would be expected, according to the Bishop of Durham, to possess "a steel cap, a coat of plate, stockings and sleeves of plate, bootes and spurres; a Skottish short sworde and a dagger, a horseman's staffe and a case of pistolls". He only needed, one would think, the buckler, or small round shield, which was also much used, to bear a striking resemblance to the White Knight in *Through the Looking Glass*. The typical reiver wore a jack, instead of a 'coat of plate', and as often as not carried a long spear or lance in place of the Jeddart staff, which was a long-handled axe carried on the shoulder. Originally, his sword was a long, two-handled

* Part spear, part axe.

affair, which perhaps explains the horizontal swipe which seems to have produced so many leg-wounds. As the sixteenth century wore on, however, this gave way to a shorter weapon which was not only easier to wield but was provided with a basketwork guard for the user's hand. An alternative to the lance and buckler was the bow; the English preferring the long-bow and the Scots the crossbow.

Rather than a case of pistols, the well-appointed reiver would prefer a single dagg, itself a larger kind of pistol. Towards the end of the period he might have invested in that ancestor of the carbine—the caliver. For long enough, however, firearms were viewed with a natural suspicion; particularly by the Scots. When the Borderers joined in the attack on Stirling and drove the Earl of Arran from James' Council, it was the spearmen to whom they ascribed their success, and not the firearms of the soldiers that accompanied them. In fact the captain of mercenaries remarked that "those who knew his soldiers as well as he did would hardly choose to march before them".

Where the foray was a sizeable one, the leader would be expected to carry, in addition to the necessary weapons, a bugle or trumpet, which was usually made of a cow's horn with hoop, chain and mouthpiece of steel.

To return, however, to the troops who were expected to take part in a warden rode. Apart from the levies of able-bodied men of the March, a warden could count on his own personal body-guard, and on the soldiery who formed the garrisons that were stationed at strategic points. Of the castles used for this purpose only Chipchase, in the valley of the North Tyne, remains complete, if very much altered, while Harbottle (in Coquetdale), Bewcastle (in Cumberland) and Norham-on-Tweed are largely ruined. On the Scottish side Hermitage still presides over Liddesdale with a majesty largely unimpaired by its lack of a roof, but Home Castle, on its 700-foot hill near Kelso, is only a modern shell and Lochmaben, on the Dumfriesshire loch of that name, a romantic skeleton.

In addition the English wardens would call on reinforcements from the garrison at Berwick, though their prayers were not always answered.

Finally there might be mercenaries. On the Scottish side these were chiefly French: on the English they were Italian, Spanish or even Greek, but principally Germans, with their clumsy firearms and uncertain discipline. These were the men, according to the Last Minstrel,

> By Conrad led of Wolfenstein,
> Who brought the band from distant Rhine,
> And sold their blood for foreign pay.

One of the many and varied dangers to which the Borders were heir was the possibility of a mutiny in the ranks of these soldiers of fortune, resulting in the appearance of roving bands whose only hope of survival lay in armed robbery.

An essential part of a warden rode was the burning of houses and of the crops that had been gathered in. The houses did not matter much as they could be quickly rebuilt or, in the case of towers, patched up, while the insight could with any luck be removed to safety. Growing crops were a different matter altogether, for without them how were the population to be fed? The loss of cattle might be a temporary annoyance which could soon be remedied by the lifting of others, and did not alter the total amount of sustenance available to the Borderers. The burning of crops did. Indeed so unpopular was it that it proved necessary on at least one occasion to enlist Irishmen to burn standing corn because, as the Earl of Hertford put it, "the Borderers will not willingly burn their neighbours".

In other respects, also, the order to take part in a warden rode must have been anything but popular. It was one thing to pursue in the heat of the moment someone who had just lifted your cattle, or to help in carrying out an act of vengeance dictated by deadly feud. It was another thing altogether to set off in cold blood to harry people who might well be allied to you or yours in marriage, or otherwise, and whose way of life, wherever they might happen to live, was much the same as your own.

To professional soldiers such a raid was almost as un-attractive as it was to the local levies, for the reivers' hideouts were as often as not protected by forest and bog, through which the safe paths, if they were not blocked with tree-trunks or the like, were imperceptible to the untrained eye. Added to the ever-present risk of ambush, therefore, was the chance of finding themselves floundering, or even drowning, in the most unpleasant of swamps, while the thieves, on their little unshod nags, cantered merrily away.

In England even large-scale reprisals could be safely left to the wardens, but in Scotland, where divided loyalties often resulted in their only wishing to leave well alone, it was an altogether different matter. The solution that seems to have commended itself to the Scottish kings was to take a hand themselves, descending upon the Borders from time to time in savage retribution.

Perhaps the best known example of such vengeance from above is to be found in the expedition of James V that resulted in the execution of Johnny Armstrong. The young king (he was only seventeen at the time) had not had time to become as cynical about Border affairs as his elders, and he was confident that all that was needed was a firm hand. He intended, he said, to "gar the rush bush keep the cow", in other words to create such a peaceful state of affairs in the Borders that brushwood, rather than force, would be required to keep a man's cattle from straying. Unfortunately he reckoned without his Uncle Henry, who was equally intent on keeping the pot boiling. So much so that he actually encouraged his wardens to trump up complaints against the Scots, and then 'devise' forays in reprisal.

So successful were these activities that by 1529 the Borders were in an uproar. Robbery, murder and arson had become so commonplace that it was almost impossible for anyone to live in peace. It was clear, therefore, to the king, if not to his advisers, that if he was to save the day he must strike quickly, and strike hard.

First he descended on the Earl of Bothwell, whose lands he seized and whose person he warded securely in Edinburgh Castle. The Lords Home and Maxwell, the lairds of Buccleuch, Ferniehirst, Polwarth and Johnstone he also warded, while requiring a number of other families to give hostages as to their good behaviour. Others were less fortunate. Cockburn of Henderland, for example, James seized on Meggat Water, accusing him of theft and of treasonably conspiring with King Henry and the Earl of Angus against the Scottish throne. Adam Scott of Tushielaw he also caught in Ettrick; the crimes with which he was charged ranging from wholesale robbery to oppression of his tenants. In particular, the King of the Borders or the King of Thieves, as Tushielaw was variously known, was accused of "theftuously taking Blackmail".

Tradition has it that both Henderland and Tushielaw were

hurried out of their own front doors and strung up, Cockburn over his own gate and Scott on the nearest tree. In fact both were taken to Edinburgh where they were tried and (in the words of Bishop Leslie) "convict thairfor and heidit, and their heidis fixit upon the Tolbuith of Edinburg". The fact that Marjorie Cockburn's husband actually lost his life in Edinburgh in no way detracts from that most moving of all ballads, 'The Border Widow's Lament', which has so often been attributed to her.

> . . . There came a man by middle day,
> He spied his sport and went away;
> And brought the king that very night,
> Who broke my bower and slew my knight.
>
> He slew my knight, to me sae dear;
> He slew my knight and poin'd* his gear;
> My servants all for life did flee,
> And left me in extremitie.
>
> I sew'd his sheet, making my mane;†
> I watch'd the corpse, myself alane;
> I watch'd his body night and day;
> No living creature came that way.
>
> I took his body on my back,
> And whiles I gaed, and whiles I sat;
> I digg'd a grave, and laid him in,
> And happ'd him with the sod sae green. . . .

The King of the Borders was a big enough fish in his own pool, but in the same net there was soon gathered a still larger one in the shape of Johnny Armstrong of Gilnockie. Johnny appears in different guises in ballads all over the North of England, as well as in his own country, and the descriptions of him have probably done more than anything else to create and perpetuate the image of the Border reiver as a 'knight in shining armour'. He was, in fact, a brother of the laird of Mangerton, chief of the Armstrong clan, and his lair overlooked the Esk near Canonbie. Legend has it that this was what is now known as Hollows Tower, but was in fact some half a mile away.

In one way or another, Johnny seems to have acquired an

* Stole.
† Moan.

importance in the Borders exceeding that of his brother and, at the time of James' expedition, he could probably call on the services of several hundred men. It may well be that a good deal of his success in life derived from the forays that he ran into England, which created such a stir that Henry (significantly, as it turned out) made a point of asking the Scottish king to bring him to heel.

After dealing so drastically with Henderland and Tushielaw, James seems to have felt the need for a little relaxation, and accordingly summoned the Earls of Huntly, Argyll and Atholl to hunt deer with him. So effective were they that the bag eventually amounted to 360 head. There is some evidence that, flushed with success, James then declared a general amnesty. Gilnockie, either trusting in this or, as tradition has it, in response to a 'loving letter' from the king inviting him to take part in the chase, set off to meet him, presumably under the impression that some kind of a safe-conduct was involved.

Before setting out, Johnny is reputed to have held a little joust with his followers on the holm of Langholm. Then, dressing himself in his Sunday best, and instructing his men to do the same, he rode away to join the royal party. On the way he was intercepted and brought with his followers before the king, not as an honoured guest, as he apparently expected, but under guard.

What the king's feelings were when Johnny was brought before him we shall presumably never know. It may well be that, as one account has it, James had originally no intention of harming Gilnockie, but that he was annoyed by the airs and graces assumed by a man whom he believed to be little more than a bandit, and that he looked on his finery, and that of his men, as clear evidence of an ambition that little became him.

> John wore a girdle about his middle,
> Imbroidered ower wi' burning gold,
> Bespangled wi' the same metal;
> Maist beautiful was to behold.

> There hang nine targets* at Johnie's hat,
> And ilk ane worth three hundred pound.
> 'What wants that knave that a king should have,
> But the sword of honour and the crown?'

* Tassels.

'O, where got thou these targets, Johnie,
That blink sae brawlie abune thy brie*?'
'I gat them in the field fechting,
Where, cruel king, thou durst not be!'

The fact that within three days, Gilnockie's estates were
awarded to Maxwell naturally raises doubts whether the latter
had not issued an apparently friendly invitation in the king's
name, but without his knowledge, and whether the whole thing
was not indeed a carefully baited trap. Whatever the explanation, it seems clear that angry words were in fact exchanged
and that orders were given for Gilnockie and his company to
be hanged forthwith.

One possible explanation of the whole puzzling episode is
that no treachery was originally intended by anyone; that a
safe conduct had in fact been offered to any malefactors who
would "submit to the king's mercy", and that Gilnockie had
relied, like so many reivers before him, on his ability to talk
himself out of a ticklish situation, rather than take the chance
of being put to the horn. James' soldiers, unaware of Johnny's
intentions, and only seeing a strong body of men armed, as
usual, to the teeth, had then taken the only prudent course
open to them and brought the Borderers to the king under
escort. It may well be that Gilnockie then adopted a high and
mighty attitude and that the king, already suspicious of his
motives, and mindful of Henry's wish to see him out of the
way, was overcome with youthful indignation.

According to the ballad, when it was finally borne in upon
Gilnockie that the king meant business, he employed the
reiver's last resort, an eloquent tongue. But it was of no
avail.

'Away, away, thou traitor strang!
Out o' my sight soon may'st thou be!
I grantit nevir a traitor's life,
And now I'll not begin wi' thee.'

But Johnny still a couple of shots in his locker. Never, he
said virtuously, had he robbed his fellow Scots. It was only on
'the auld enemy' that he had preyed. "King Harry," he said,
"would down weigh my best horse with gold to know that I
was condemned to die this day". He was not far wrong for,

* Brow.

in the words of the chronicler, "the English people were exceeding glad that Johnny Armstrong was executed".

In the circumstances, this plea probably did Johnny more
harm than good, for James was not at war with England, and
the fact that one of his subjects was in the habit of attacking
an allegedly friendly neighbour was an aggravation rather than
an excuse. Nor was James likely to listen with much sympathy
to Gilnockie's final proposition. It was well known that he was
running a thriving protection racket on the other side of the
Border, and now he offered to cut the king in on it.

> 'Grant me my life, my liege, my king!
> And a brave gift I'll gie to thee—
> All between here and Newcastle town
> Sall pay their yeirly rent to thee.'

But James was adamant, and Gilnockie had to admit defeat.

> 'To seek het water beneith cauld ice,
> Surely it is a great folie—
> I have asked grace at a graceless face,
> But there is nane for my men and me.'

And so, for better or for worse, Gilnockie and his retinue
were hanged, twelve of them, it is believed, in Edinburgh, but
the rest of them on the spot—that is to say, at Carlenrig, a
mile or so west of Teviothead, some ten miles along the road
from Hawick to Langholm. Here there is to be seen the old
churchyard, a serene oasis of close-cropped grass and ancient
tombstones, almost surrounded by trees, where tradition has
it that Johnny Armstrong and his men now lie in peace.

But if King James thought that, as a result, the state of the
Borders might improve, he was sorely mistaken. All that happened was that the last traces of loyalty to the crown were
extinguished, while many of the Armstrongs migrated to
Cumberland whence they resumed their reiving with a vigour
that was only intensified by the treatment their surname had
received.

When Tushielaw was accused of "theftuously taking blackmail", the word was being used in the original sense, for it was
here in the Borders that it was first coined. Rent, or tribute,
was commonly known in Scotland as 'mail', so that grassmail

represented money paid out for grazing, and 'to pay the mail' meant to pay atonement. Blackmail, then, signified an illegal rent, as when Gilnockie promised King James that, if his life were spared, the English should "pay their yeirly rent to thee". In fact, it was a protection racket.

It was the Grahams who developed blackmail from mere opportunism into a regular business, employing narks to make regular collections on their behalf. Thus Richie Graham of Brackenhill is to be found ordering his factor, William Hayer, to despoil sundry Hetheringtons and others who had failed to pay their protection money. The queen's tenants in Leven, the younger Scrope reported, were regularly paying twenty shillings per annum to the Grahams, but no rent to the queen. Moreover, while they had previously "served her with horse and gear", they were now doing the Grahams' carting instead.

Hutchen Graham was another shrewd operator. When, for instance, he was arrested in 1606, one of the offences with which he was charged was that, three years ago

> he brought one hundred and forty of his kinsmen and friends, English and Scottish, to the town of Cargo near Carlisle and provided them with victuals for themselves and their horses, free of cost, at the charge of the town. He had for many years taken this town into his protection, receiving from each husbandman four pecks of malt yearly for black mail, these pecks being of Carlisle measure, twenty gallons to the bushel.

When taxed with extortion, the Grahams were profuse in their explanations. On one occasion the payments were alleged to represent rewards for protecting their clients against the enemy (which was near enough to the truth, if not to the whole truth). On another,

> they deny receiving any [blackmail] but in satisfaction of money laid out in redemption of the tenants' goods with their own consents, which could be recovered no other way for want of a warden in the Scottish Middle Marches.

The usual method of exacting blackmail was to threaten to take a man's stock, or burn his house and insight, if he did not make regular payments either in money or kind. In return the blackmailer would promise his protection against the depredations of others. A variation on this theme is to be found in the account of a Scottish foray which, in 1558, penetrated as far south as Morpeth. Here the reivers roused the various inhabitants by name but, instead of threatening what they themselves would do, told them that a whole army of Scots were approaching, who would undoubtedly take all their gear. If the victim would give his hand through the window and swear to be a true prisoner of the blackmailer, and appear when required in order to pay the agreed price, he would be left alone.

Blackmail depended for its success on two factors. The first, ironically enough, was the Borderer's insistence on keeping his word, which laid him open to a system of extortion which otherwise could hardly have survived. The second was the way in which everyone seems to have known everyone else's name. It is true that the blackmailer would probably announce himself and so ensure that there was no doubt about his identity. What is not so easy to understand is how, when he came from the other side of the Border, he so often knew the name of the victim, even allowing for the extent to which the two nationalities intermingled at markets, race meetings, football matches and days of truce. Still more difficult to fathom is how, when one reiver approached a steading, he was to know that it was under the protection of another. In the majority of cases he probably did not, so that the only value of the protection offered lay in helping the owner to reclaim his goods, once they had been lifted.

(*right*) Hollows, a tower of the Armstrongs near Gilnockie. (*below*) "A cheaper alternative to the stone tower"—Gatehouse Bastle in the valley of the Tarset Burn.

(*left*) The Bastle House at The Hole, near West Woodburn in Redesdale. (*below*) "The ceiling of this ground floor was vaulted . . . like a railway tunnel, and pierced by a trap door." Hole Bastle.

CHAPTER SEVEN

The Border Way of Life

Lock the door, Larriston, lion of Liddesdale,
Lock the door, Larriston, Lowther comes on;
The Armstrongs are flying,
The widows are crying,
The Castletown's burning and Oliver's gone.

James Hogg, 'Larriston of Liddesdale'

Border history is full of stories of 'towns' being burnt or destroyed; usually by reivers but often on the instructions of a warden. "Ding down the nests", wrote the Earl of Angus, "and the rooks'll flee away". But the rooks did not fly away; they waited for their assailants to depart, and then rebuilt. As Patten, the historian of Somerset's expedition into Scotland, observed, they would "the next day make other and not remove from the ground, so wretchedly could they live and endure the pain that no Englishman could suffer the like. The Englishman could, however, and did, for south of the Border his plight was much the same as it would have been in Scotland.

The first thing to do was to plant a few stakes in the ground. The gaps were filled in with stones and divots of turf, and the walls finished off in 'rice and gloor' (that is to say, brushwood and mud) or, as it was known in Scotland, 'cat and clay'. Branches were then laid across to make a roof but, unlike the cottages of the Scottish Highlands where the smoke was just allowed to percolate through the heather thatch, a smoke hole was provided. The windows were unglazed, but wooden shutters were provided for use in stormy weather, or at night; while the door was usually made of cowhide.

Three or four hours were generally considered enough time to erect these cabins. To build anything better would have been futile, seeing that it might well be destroyed again on the morrow. Indeed if a house had taken much longer to erect, the owner might well have died of exposure before it was completed. So ingrained did this habit of living in hastily-built shanties become that, in the reign of Charles I, it was still possible for a stranger to describe Belford as "the most beggarly town of sods that was made in the afternoon of loam and sticks".

Pennant, writing in 1771 nearly two centuries after the heyday of the reivers, commented that most of the houses in Canonbie were still built of clay. Anyone wishing to build a house "then summons his neighbours on a fixed day, who come furnished with victuals at their own expense, set cheerfully to work, and complete the edifice before night".

The better houses sometimes had a half-wall of stone, and were then completed in the same way as the others. If no stone was readily available, wooden shuttering was used, into which wet clay was tamped, interspersed with straw. In general, however, the Borderers' houses, as described by Leslie, were "sheephouses and lodges . . . of whose burning they are not sore solaced". The entrance, as often as not, would be through the byre in which the cattle were tied, while divots were preferred for the roof as being less inflammable than rushes or heather. When Lord Eure, on a raid into Scotland in 1588, detached a number of his soldiery to burn Eyemouth Mill, they returned in high dudgeon to report that "the mill was turfed and would not burn well".

Dwellings like these might afford some protection from the weather, but virtually none from the inhumanity of man. Such defence as there was came from the 'peels' built by the lairds for the benefit of themselves and their dependants. Words tend to change their meaning as time goes on, and sometimes quite rapidly. It is not surprising, therefore, that the word 'peel' (often spelt 'pele') has been used at different times to identify a variety of defensive arrangements. From time immemorial, stockades of different kinds had been used, as for instance in Cumberland, where were "the circles of very old thorns, or . . . other inclosures which the people of each village or hamlet used to collect and watch their cattle by night for fear of a surprise; these are called lodges".

The next step seems to have been the replacement of the

thorns by a wooden palisade, to which 'bratishes', or timber screens, might be added. As time went on, it was discovered that brushwood and clay were acceptable alternatives to wood, particularly as the result was less inflammable; and that a wall of turf and clay, reinforced by timber, was better still. Known sometimes as a 'fill-dyke', this was further strengthened by the soil from a ditch being heaped against it; the ditch itself being filled, if possible, with water. The whole fortified area thus created was named, after the pales of which the palisade was originally constructed, a 'pele' or 'peel'.

Such a primitive 'strength', however suitable for the stock for which it was originally designed, provided little shelter for its owners. Inside the stockyard, therefore, was erected a primitive 'tower', built like the surrounding wall, of turf and clay reinforced with timber, with sloping sides. Wherever possible, this tower was erected on inclined ground, so that the ladder which led directly to the first floor need not be so steep as to preclude the aged and the very young from entering. Into the ground floor could be driven the most valuable of the stock.

A further stage in the development of what was rapidly becoming a minor fortress was the substitution of stone and mortar for timber and clay and, by the middle of the sixteenth century, stone towers were becoming fairly common. The same requirement to provide even stronger defences also led to the use of stone for the outer stockade, which then became known as a 'barmkin'. The Privy Council of Scotland at one time actually issued an edict instructing all men of substance to build barmkins of stone and lime, sixty feet square, while lesser men were to construct 'peels and great strengths' within which their stock and those of their tenants or neighbours could similarly be driven.

The word 'peel' then, was originally used to describe the whole fortress, and subsequently, as is shown by the requirement of the Privy Council, a fortification of timber and clay as distinct from one of stone. It was not until well into the seventeenth century that the tower belonging to a peel, or even the tower within a barmkin, became known as a peel tower. Eventually, and quite erroneously, any Border tower came itself to be known as a peel.

Another source of confusion has been the meaning of the word 'barmkin'. It is quite clear that, originally, it denoted a stone wall surrounding the yard into which the stock were driven. The use of the expression 'within the barmkin', how-ever, soon led to the courtyard itself being known as such, and the two meanings have been pretty well interchangeable ever since.

The possession of a tower did not, of course, remove the risk of fire to which other dwellings were subject: it only reduced it, and various methods were tried in order to lessen the danger. The survey of 1541, for instance, describes the houses of the hedesmen of Tynedale as being made from great strong oak trees cut square, strongly bound together and covered with thick roofs of turf and earth, which were difficult to break down or burn. Bishop Leslie commented that many of the Scots made "towers of earth which can not be burnt, nor without great force of men of war down can be cast".

A cheaper alternative to the stone tower was the 'bastle', or 'bastle house' (from the French *bastille* a fortified place). As can be seen from the examples at Akeld, near Wooler, at Gate-house in North Tynedale and at The Hole, in Redesdale, these buildings are longer, narrower and lower than a tower: in fact, fortified houses rather than miniature castles. The walls are perhaps five or six feet thick, compared to ten feet or more; entrance to the first floor is by external stone steps and there is no trace of a barmkin; stock being accommodated only in the vaulted 'pend'.

When the Earl and Countess of Northumberland sought refuge with Jock o' the Side after the abortive Rising of the North, the Countess' ladies commented, rather ungratefully, that his house in Liddesdale "was a cottage not to be compared with any dog-kennel in England". In fact this may well have been the farmhouse which Jock would only vacate in favour of his tower when forced to do so. The tower itself, more suited to defence than comfort, would probably have been much like those which Christopher Lowther encountered on his journey into Scotland after the Union. "The houses of the Grahams," he wrote, "are but one little stone tower, garreted and slated, or thatched, some of the form of a little tower not garreted, such be all the Lairds' houses in Scotland".

The typical tower was a solid, square mass of local grey stone, perhaps forty by fifty feet in plan, but very much smaller inside. The earlier, and grander, towers were built of dressed stone and often rose to a height of five, or even six, storeys. Later on, as protective towers became more common, they would rarely exceed three storeys of partly-dressed material with huge corner stones. In the whole of a wall the admission of light and air might be limited to a few arrow slits and possibly one window. The pend (in other words the ground floor) took the form, as in the bastle house, of a large stable or byre into which the milking cows and the more valuable of the horses could be driven, and was surrounded by stone storage bins. The ceiling of this ground floor was vaulted in such a way as to look, to modern eyes, rather like a railway tunnel. It was pierced by a trap-door, perhaps two-and-a-half feet square, through which a man might pass in order to feed and water the animals and milk the cows when the door was barred against the enemy.

On the next, or living, floor were the main hall, the kitchen and the dining hall, in which the menfolk also slept. A huge fireplace probably took up most of one wall, surmounted by an equally vast chimney, tapering up to the roof. One, or more, of the windows, devoid of glass but shuttered against the Border winds, were often bowed out on the inside to accommodate stone window seats, and in these 'shot windows', as they were called, the ladies of the house could sit when they were not in their small unheated rooms on the second floor.

Above the bedrooms came the steeply pitched roof, covered with thatch or, preferably, stone slabs. Here there would be a 'clan bell' on which to give the alarm, as well as the grid in which a beacon would burn. Round the roof proper ran a narrow passage within the battlements, bearing more stone seats on which the ladies could, on rare occasions, sun themselves, and this, in turn, connected with the 'bartizans', or platforms built over the corners of the tower. These were sometimes made of wood, but more usually of stone, and were pierced to allow the defenders to drop stones, boiling water or anything else they could dream up, onto the enemy below.

In the vast thickness of the tower wall or, on occasion, in an excrescence built for the purpose, was a 'turnpike', or spiral staircase. This would normally turn in a clockwise direction so that a defender's sword-arm would be free, but that of the attacker restricted. Except, of course, in the case of the Kers for, like the tribe of Benjamin,

> They were all bred left-handed men
> And fence against them there was none.

In towers belonging to the Kers themselves, therefore, the staircase normally turned anti-clockwise.

Between the foot of the stair and the outside world were two doors; the outer a heavy oaken affair closely studded with nails, and the inner a 'yett' or gate in the form of a strong iron grid. These would be reinforced by a heavy beam of wood which might extend up to five feet into the length of the wall on either side.

A fine example of the smaller type of tower is to be found at Smailholm, between Melrose and Kelso. Standing on a hill with crags on three sides and what remains of the surrounding loch on the other, the tower was built in the fifteenth century, of blue whinstone, four storeys high with walls nine feet thick. The remains of the barmkin wall, which enclosed a small chapel as well as the tower itself, are still to be seen. As so often, there is but a single window in the whole of the north wall, while bartizans, winding staircase and vaulted ground floor complete with trap-door, are altogether typical.

In the south wall is the entrance, which was defended by an iron yett with a bolt no less than three inches in diameter. Then follows a tiny barbican, nine feet (that is to say, the thickness of the wall) in length, before the inner door is reached. On the second and third floors are large fireplaces, stone window seats and garderobes.*

An older, and more ambitious, type is to be found in Cocklaw Tower, near Chollerton, in North Tynedale, which is representative of the miniature castles rather than the towers that were later built on both sides of the Border. Forty feet by fifty, and built of huge ashlar blocks, its entrance is, once more, in the south wall, which in this case is no less than fifteen feet thick. A door to the right of it leads to the spiral stairway in the thickness of the wall, while opposite lies a guardroom and a narrow dungeon, the only entrance to which originally was a trapdoor in the ceiling. Another building, probably a chapel, was approached by a further door.

---

* The medieval lavatory.

The size of the windows marks the difference between this 'residential' castle and the less habitable towers that followed. So does the dungeon, which gave way in later buildings to the more mundane cattle-shelter. The former would often have been what was known as an 'oubliette', from the French *oublier* (to forget). That this was a well chosen name for a prison to which there was no proper door is supported by the story of Archie Armstrong, who was captured on one of his cattle-raiding expeditions by Sir Thomas Swinburne, and immured in such a dungeon in Haughton Castle (also in North Tynedale). Sir Thomas then set off for York, quite forgetting to give orders for the prisoner to be fed. By the time that he remembered and returned post-haste to the castle, the unfortunate Armstrong had starved to death.

Within the barmkin, and in addition to the tower, and possibly a chapel, there might also be provided 'mansions' for the laird and his family in time of peace, and buildings to house the servants. No shelter would normally be provided for the animals left outside the tower, and it has been suggested that, in Scotland at any rate, this was because its provision might have been thought to emulate the nobility, with their stables in the castle courtyard.

For many of the lairds the tower was the only home they knew, however uncomfortable it may have appeared to south-country gentry who, in Tudor times, were busy building unfortified manor houses in which they could enjoy the luxuries of peace. The traveller, William Harrison, poured scorn on the increasingly luxurious habits of the south-country English. "When our houses were builded of willow," he wrote, "then had we oaken men, but now that our houses are come to be made of oak, our men are not only become as willows, but a great many altogether of straw which is a sore alteration." The Border lairds were very far from being men of straw, but there were many of them who, if they could afford it, preferred to spend as much time as possible in a farm house, while keeping their tower as a refuge to which they could send their wives and children in emergency, only garrisoning it fully if they feared a prolonged raid. Thus Sir Robert Carey writes during his term as Scrope's deputy, of one of the Grahams having "a pretty house, and close to it a strong tower for his own defence in time of need".

When the beacons signalled that a raid was on the way, the laird, and those of his dependents who could conveniently do so, would waste no time in driving their stock within the barmkin and themselves going to ground in the tower. Meanwhile, the remainder of the population took to the hills and forests, together with their animals and belongings, and lay low till all was over. The insight that the cottagers possessed would amount to very little, and what there was could easily be carried away or hidden or, in the case of furniture, replaced if it were burnt. Such furniture would probably be no more than a 'lang settle' or two with, perhaps, an awning to keep the soot, or leaks from the roof, from the goodman's head; with three-legged stools for the lads and lasses, and 'crackets'* for the bairns and old women. In places where wood was scarce even the roof beams were made removable so that, at Bamburgh for instance, they accompanied the cottagers into the castle.

The houses and towers of the lairds were, of course, a great deal better furnished, even if they lagged behind the standards of the south. Window glass was hardly to be found, for it was so expensive that when the Earls of Northumberland left Alnwick for one of their other seats, the panes were all taken out of the windows and either taken with them or stored away for safety's sake. Walls were sometimes plastered and decorated, but tapestries were few and far between. Turkey carpets were just becoming fashionable in the North towards the end of the period, but were used to cover walls and tables rather than floors, where moor-grass, birch twigs and rushes, mixed with sweet-smelling heather, thyme or yellow bedstraw, were used. If changed frequently enough, they would prove a delightful substitute. If not, as foreigners sometimes complained, they might prove quite the reverse.

In view of the ever-present danger of one's home and insight being burnt, tower furniture was kept to a minimum. Not only were window seats, for instance, made of stone, but other items also, such as the sloping stone panels which acted as bookrests, as in the Vicar's Tower at Corbridge. Chairs, on the whole, were a rarity. The laird would insist on one, as befitting his position, and some might have two or more. In general, however, chests, settles and stools took their place. In the

* More a small low bench than a stool.

earlier part of the sixteenth century, bedsteads were still considered the height of luxury, but the more affluent might sleep on feather mattresses (or beds as they were known) and others either on flock or on palliasses of straw.

Despite the general tendency towards greater luxury, the ever-present danger of fire and 'spulzie'* saw to it that the furnishings of Border towers remained spartan. Blankets, cushions, pillows and tablecloths appear in their inventories, but little else that could be described by any stretch of the imagination as luxuries. The remainder of the insight that a Borderer owned would be in the shape of clothing which would usually be of the simplest, though the better off might indulge in finery which contrasted curiously with their normal way of life.

Whereas William Aynsley of East Shaftoe, for instance, left in his will "two jackets, two doublets, two pairs of hose, four shirts, one hat and one Spanish cap", Sir George Heron's will in 1575 included "a damask gown, a velvet jerkin, a pair of velvet breeches and a satin doublet". Of underclothes there is no mention at all; perhaps, as was once the case with slum children, people's under-garments were sewn on and removed only at rare intervals.

Patten, when he accompanied Somerset's expedition against the Scots, took particular notice of the similarity in dress of the Scottish lairds to that of their followers. Lairds and barons, he remarked, wore not only the same jacks, covered with white leather, as their men, but the same white leather or fustian doublets and, usually, white hose. This, he said, explained why so many of the 'great men' were killed in action. At first sight, this seems a strange observation to make, for one might have thought exactly the opposite would have been the case. The explanation, no doubt, is that if they had stood out from the mass, their lives would have been spared in the hope of a swingeing ransom.

Normally, a reiver would not have been very much concerned with his appearance, for his business was strictly utilitarian. Yet for his wife he was usually anxious to provide what finery he could, of which she would be inordinately proud.

The food that he ate, when at home, seems to have consisted mainly of meat, cheese, and barley that had been either parched

* Plundering.

or boiled. Bread he enjoyed but rarely and, when he did, it was likely also to be made of barley, possibly filled out with peas or beans. White bread the typical reiver would not encounter at all, nor any kind of wine, though the gentry were well acquainted with both, particularly claret. Drunkenness appears to have been fairly rare at any level, and only one instance of a nickname reflecting such a state comes readily to mind and that was given to John Bell, known as the Bendar because of the frequency with which he became 'cup-shotten'.

Vegetables must have been in short supply, for potatoes were still (in the sixteenth century) unknown in the Borders, and cabbages new-fangled. Mary Queen of Scots complained that on her escape from the battle of Langside she had been "three nights like the owls", drinking only sour milk and eating "oat-meal without bread". Yet, only half a century later, Christopher Lowther was regaled at Langholm with mutton, chicken, oat-cakes and wheaten bread, washed down with ale and aqua vitae. It was a far cry, indeed, from the present that Valentine Browne, when he was Treasurer at Berwick, once sent to Robert Cecil, in the shape of "a box containing the puddings of a solan goose of Scotland".

The rations of a reiver when on his unlawful occasions, as distinct from what he may have eaten at home, were probably much the same as those attributed by Froissart to Scottish soldiers of the fifteenth century. They had no need, he said, of pots and pans for they "dress the flesh of cattle in their skins after they have taken them off". Then he goes on, "Under the flaps of his saddle each man carries a broad plate of metal, behind the saddle a little bag of oatmeal. When they have eaten too much of the sodden flesh, and their stomach sems weak and empty, they place the plate over the fire, mix with water their oatmeal, and when the plate is heated, they put a little of the paste upon it and make a thin cake like a cracknel or biscuit, which they eat to warm their stomachs".

By way of indoor recreation, the reivers were much given to poetry and music, the two being more or less inseparable; for when they were not playing the smallpipes they were sing-ing the ballads of the Border to the accompaniment of harp or pipe. So much was this a part of their life that it comes as something of a shock to find a traveller in Tweeddale comment-ing that there "Musick is so great a stranger that you shall hardly light upon a one amongst three that can distinguish one tune from another".

The poetry in question, which took the form of epics handed down by word of mouth, was nearly always tragic, with occasional flashes of humour but few happy endings. It was the stark realities of life—and death—of which the reivers sang. In the words of George Macaulay Trevelyan (himself a Borderer),

The Border people wrote the Border ballads. Like the Homeric Greeks, they were cruel, coarse savages, slaying each other as beasts of the forest, and yet they were also poets who could express in the grand style the inexorable fate of the individual man and woman. It was not one ballad maker alone but the whole cut-throat population who felt this magnanimous sorrow. . . .

Perhaps this melancholy was inevitable. Dr Johnson is reputed to have said to the unfortunate Dr Dodd, who had been sentenced to death for forgery, "Depend upon it, sir, if a man is to be hanged in a fortnight, it concentrates his mind wonderfully".

Music and poetry, however, were by no means the reiver's only relaxation. During the hours of darkness, when the wind howled round farmstead and tower, and there was no particular incentive to 'ride', he might while away the time playing cards, of which he was passionately fond. Gambling, indeed, was in his very blood, which is hardly to be wondered at considering how often he was forced to risk his life in the course of business. Many a horse and beast, the profit of a moonlight foray, must have changed hands in this way; in throwing dice and in the enjoyment of the 'tables'* which featured so often in the inventories of the gentry.

For those same gentry, hawking and hunting, especially of red deer, provided suitable exercise and recreation when not engaged in reiving or in fighting each other. So much so that it became usual, when times were quiet, for Scotsmen to ask leave to cross the Border and hunt in the Forest of Cheviot and elsewhere. During the last years of Sir John Forster's wardenship of the Middle March, however, the Scots began to take advantage of his age and growing lethargy to hunt without

* Backgammon board.

permission, and furthermore to cut wood and take it back to Scotland, an exercise which was expressly forbidden by the Border Laws. They caught a Tartar, nevertheless, a few years after Forster's removal, when a large party crossed the Border into Redesdale, and Sir Robert Carey, a warden of a very different stamp, was informed of what was happening and rode out to meet them. When asked why they had crossed the Border without leave, the Scots answered that they were peace-fully hunting deer, and what was all the fuss about? Carey, seeing that they were "eighty or more, armed with calivers and horsemen's pieces" which were quite unsuitable for the chase, begged leave to differ, and the 'hunt' soon became a battle.

After this, Carey made it known once more that there was no objection to the Scots coming into England for the purposes of sport so long as they asked his permission. He might have saved his breath, for it was not long before he discovered them once again combining business with pleasure by hunting on the English side (again without leave) and then carrying away cart-loads of fuel. He succeeded in catching "twelve of the principal gentlemen and breaking their carts". Then, to everyone's surprise, he proceeded to entertain these same gentlemen at Widdrington Castle, before allowing them to return whence they came. This enlightened action, so typical of the new warden's commonsense approach to his problems, seems to have abated this particular nuisance. The Scots began to ask his leave once more, and Carey actually joined in their hunts, to the evident pleasure of Queen Elizabeth, if not of James, who seems to have had reservations. It was only a few years later that John Johnstone of Gretna was again asking leave to hunt deer on the English side, in order that the chief of his surname could celebrate his daughter's christening with venison; a request that the Keeper of Tynedale was pleased to grant.

While the gentry hunted and hawked, lesser men coursed hares, until an English law of 1605 limited the sport to forty-shilling freeholders. Football was enjoyed by all classes, and no doubt it proved a useful safety valve for energies that might otherwise have found less innocent outlets. The Scottish authorities, finding that the pastime interfered with archery practice, banned it at one time, together with the game of golf; while allowing bowls, ninepins, cards, dice and 'tables'.

The Armstrongs of Liddesdale were particularly fond of matching their football skills with those of other surnames, including those of Tynedale, in games which sometimes lasted from dawn to dusk, interrupted only by free fights and broken limbs. The game was usually played by as many on either side as cared to join in, though a restriction of numbers was not unknown. A star player was Wat Armstrong, who finally met his end in a raid on Haltwhistle. It was Alec Ridley, one of a famous riding surname in those parts,

> . . . who lette flee
> A clothyard shaft ahint the wa';
> It struck Wat Armstrong in the 'ee,
> Went through his steel cap, heed and a',
> I wot it made him quickly fa'.
> He cudna' rise tho' he essayed,
> The best at thieve craft or the ba',
> He ne'er again shall ride a raid.

A considerable exponent of the game was the fifth Earl of Bothwell, the nephew and successor of the earl who had married Mary Queen of Scots. Apparently he was not averse to tripping, and perhaps to ankle-tapping as well, for "Some quarrel happened the other day", wrote Robert Bowes from the Scottish court, "betwixt Bothwell and the Master of Marischal upon a stroke given at football upon Bothwell's leg by the master after that the Master had received a sore fall by Bothwell".

It was in 1599 that some of the Armstrongs of Whithaugh proposed the first six-a-side match known to history, which was duly played at Bewcastle. One of the Ridleys, hearing that these "great thieves and arch murderers" might be theirs for the asking, assembled a party of his relations and friends and set out to capture them, with what fell intent we do not know. Francis Forster of Kershope Foot, however, overheard the plotters and persuaded two women to take a warning message to the Armstrongs, whom they found on the field of play. The footballers were accordingly enabled to arrange an ambush in which they cut the throats of Ridley and of Nichol Welton, killed one of the Robsons and took no less than thirty prisoners.

It was at a football match, also, in the year 1600, that the final arrangements were made to murder a Scottish warden. This was Sir John Carmichael, one of the principals in 'the unhappy accident' of the Redeswire who, perhaps because he was not a Borderer himself, had made quite a reputation as Warden of the West March. In so doing, however, he not unnaturally made many enemies among the reivers, and particularly the Armstrongs. Knowing that the warden had in mind to punish his tribe for their latest exploits, and hoping to get his oar in first, Ringan Armstrong set off to remonstrate with Carmichael.

Unfortunately, some of the warden's staff began to make fun of Ringan and managed to take his sword from the scabbard and to pour in yolk-of-egg, which made it virtually impossible for him to draw. So incensed was the hedesman at this treatment that he swore that the next time his sword left its resting place it would be in earnest. Accordingly Thomas Armstrong, variously described as the son of Ringan's Thom and of Sandy's Thom, organized "at ane meeting at the futeball" an expedition to waylay Carmichael as he rode next day to hold a warden's court at Lochmaben. All went according to plan and at a place known as Raesknowes, some six miles to the west of Langholm, on the road to Lockerbie and Lochmaben, the Armstrongs "schott their hagbuts" at him and the warden fell dead.

Thomas Armstrong was soon run to earth, taken to the Mercat Cross in Edinburgh and hanged, but not before his right hand had been struck off, presumably because it had fired the fatal shot.

For long enough, the rest of the murderers defied all the authorities' efforts to bring them to book; the Privy Council deciding, with a curious sense of priorities, that one of them, Sandy of Rowanburn, "has ever been a common and notorious thief, trained up from his youth in reif, theft and oppression according to the accustomed trade of the wicked and unhappy race of his father's gang* and branch", and should be punished. He was to be tried "for the crimes of theft and reif or any other crimes whereof they can get sufficient information . . . against him, and failing thereof for the shameful and cruel murder of . . . Sir John Carmichael of that Ilk . . . committed by his father, brother and the rest of that branch."

* Grayne.

It is to this Sandy Armstrong, on the eve of his execution, that tradition ascribes 'Armstrong's Goodnight'.

This night is my departing night,
For here nae longer maun I stay;
There's neither friend nor foe o' mine
But wishes me away.

What I hae done through lack o' wit
I never, never, can recall;
I hope ye're a' my friends as yet,
Goodnight, and joy be wi' ye all.

Of all the recreations in which the reivers indulged, it was probably horse-racing in which they found their greatest fulfil-ment. In an occupation where a man's life might well depend on the speed and staying power of his mount, the horse assumed an importance that can hardly be over-estimated, and to own the best, and prove as much in competition with his fellows, was something that every reiver naturally desired. A race-meeting not only satisfied this urge but also provided an admirable opportunity for gambling.

While horse races were held at Berwick, in Teviotdale and elsewhere, it was in the West Marches of England that they seem to have been most popular. Such places as Langwathby Moor and Kingsmoor, for instance, were not only within easy reach of the citizens of Carlisle, but also of Scotsmen anxious to do a little illegal trafficking in horses, and particularly Thomas Sandford's famous breed. There is no evidence that any money prizes were offered at these meetings and, as every Borderer would be prepared to back his own horse, there was probably no need. The winner was rewarded, however, with a bell, which took the place of a cup.

There were three Scotsmen in particular who seem to have found these Cumberland meetings irresistible—the Laird of Mangerton, his kinsman Kinmont Willie, and the footballing Earl of Bothwell. In 1585, for instance, when both Musgraves and Carletons were strongly suspected of treasonable dealings with Mangerton and the rest of the Armstrongs, it was thought that the gift of a racehorse formed part of the deal. On Easter Tuesday Humfrey Musgrave's Bay Sandforth ran at a meeting in Liddesdale so that Mangerton could assess his value. The horse won all three bells and, sure enough, appeared next in

Mangerton's colours. The Armstrongs, including Kinmont, then returned with Thomas Carleton to his official residence at Askerton, "ranne the bell of the Wainrigge" and stayed the night at Naworth, where Kinmont bought a horse from Lancelot Carleton called Grey Carver. All this, not only at a time when international horse-dealing was forbidden, but when Kinmont was virtually proscribed. It was in 1600 that the latter was in the news once more, when one of Thomas Sandford's horses was stolen from his stud at Howgill. Sir Richard Lowther reported that Kinmont had bought the mare from "two or three limmer thieves" and was riding her himself.

It was racing, moreover, among other amusements, that served to pass away the time for Bothwell when he had made Scotland too hot to hold him. As a guest of Walter Graham at Netherby, he seems to have consoled himself mainly by attending meetings in order to indulge in his passion for betting, and in playing cards with Balfour of Burleigh, whom Lowther described as "another of our declared traitors".

(*above*) Haughton Castle, in North Tynedale, where Archie Armstrong starved to death. (*below*) "A fine example of the smaller type of tower is to be found at Smailholm."

(*above*) "Sloping stones which acted as bookrests, as in the case of the Vicar's Tower at Corbridge." (*left*) "The Queen's House" at Jedburgh in which Mary Queen of Scots lay ill after riding to Hermitage to visit the wounded Bothwell.

CHAPTER EIGHT

The Reivers Foul their Own Nests

Some die ganging, and some die hanging,
And a twine of a tow for me, my dear,
And a twine of a tow for me.
A. C. Swinburne, 'A Reiver's Neck Verse'

Throughout the sixteenth century the wardens on both sides of the Border were wont to complain of 'the great familiarity between the people of the two countries'. One might be forgiven for thinking that in times of peace, or at any rate in the absence of official warfare, such friendliness would have been welcome; but this would be to misunderstand the problems with which the wardens were confronted. At any moment war might break out, or a punitive raid become necessary; in which case, although the Borderers were happy to fight each other for their own ends, their natural cussedness would become evident. They might be led, but on no account would they be driven; least of all by officialdom to whom they were naturally allergic. Still less could they be forced to do battle against those to whom they might be allied by ties of friendship, and particularly of marriage.

In his history of Somerset's campaign, for instance, Patten describes how the Borderers wore handkerchiefs on their arms and letters on their caps which, he had a strong suspicion, were used for purposes of individual recognition by the enemy, and "so in conflict either each to spare other or gently each to take other". Moreover, the crosses of St Andrew or St George, as the case might be, that were worn on their white surcoats, were "so narrow and so singly set on that a puff of wind might have blown them from their breasts".

Even without intermarriage, which the authorities constantly strove to discourage, it was often difficult to know on whose side a particular surname might be operating. "They are a people," wrote Thomas Musgrave, "that will be Scottish when they will and English at their pleasure." The Bishop of Carlisle was of the same opinion, and once complained to Wolsey that

> there is more theft, more extortion by English thieves than there is by all the Scots of Scotland . . . for in Hexham . . . every market day there is four score or a hundred strong thieves; and the poor men and gentlemen also seeeth them which did rob them and their goods, and dare neither complain of them by name, nor say one word to them. They take all their cattle and horse, their corn as they carry it to sow, or to the mill to grind, and at their houses bid them deliver what they will have or they shall be fired and burnt.

The objects of the Bishop's complaint on this occasion were the reivers of Tynedale, but the surname that, without doubt, caused him more anguish than any other were the Grahams, a clan with a soul above nationality and an eye directed almost exclusively to the main chance. Living, as they did, in and around the Debatable Lands, they obeyed no master unless it happened to suit them.

According to family tradition, the Grahams had been banished from Scotland, and originally settled along the banks of Leven*, between Solport and its junction with the Esk. Subsequently the Storys, fleeing from the warden's wrath, moved into Northumberland and the Grahams took their lands. By the middle of the sixteenth century they were able to call on five hundred armed men under Lang William Graham of Stubhill, to whose son, Fergus of the Mote, arms were granted some three years later. By the end of the century it was estimated that Rob Graham alone commanded "two or three thousand men useful to England".

Not only did intermarriage and self-interest enable the Grahams, from their base in the Debatable Lands, to be useful to England or to Scotland at will, but their loyalties, such as they were, seem to have been curiously divided even among themselves. John Graham, for example, who was in the habit of taking his troubles to the Privy Council of Scotland, complained on one occasion that "Dick Graham, Englishman", had

* Now Lyne.

raided his house at Canonbie—in other words, Richard Graham
of Netherby.

Robbery, murder, blackmail and kidnapping; the Grahams
indulged in them all : a famous example of the latter being the
exploit of that murderous ruffian, Jock of the Peartree. It so
happened that in the closing years of Thomas, Lord Scrope's
wardenship. Peartree's brother Wattie was caught in the act
of stealing a horse in the county of Westmorland, and found
himself in Appleby gaol. Whereupon, Peartree conceived the
idea of kidnapping the little son of Salkeld, the sheriff of
Cumberland, and exchanging him for Wattie. When riding past
Corby Castle, near Carlisle, one day, he was lucky enough to
come upon the child playing outside. In time-honoured fashion,
Peartree offered him an apple and, having succeeded with his
opening gambit, asked, "Master, will you ride?" Master was
delighted, but not so pleased when he found himself shut up in
a Graham tower waiting to be exchanged. The transaction was
duly arranged and the two Grahams re-united in their life of
crime.

As if the activities of the Grahams were not bad enough, the
wardens of the West March of England had also to contend
with the Carletons. It might have been expected that, holding
as they did a number of official positions, they would have been
on the side of the angels. Instead, they used the power, and
more particularly the knowledge, they enjoyed, to feather their
own nests, not so much by engaging in open robbery and
violence as by encouraging others, and especially the Armstrongs, to do their dirty work for them. In this they were ably
assisted by the Lowthers, who were just as jealous of the
wardens' position as they were.

It was soon after the release of Kinmont that Scrope, who
had suffered at the Carletons' hands more than most, began to
see a ray of light. "Yesterday," he wrote, "old Gerard Lowther
departed this transitory life to go and yield an account of his
stewardship in the Sovereign Court." If he thought that this
spelt the end of the unholy alliance between the Lowthers and
the Carletons, and therefore that he could at last look forward
to a little loyalty from his staff, he was to be sharply dis-
illusioned. In fact it was not long before Scrope was constrained
to report that that worthy gentleman, Mr Edward Aglionby,
had been found murdered at his home, Drawdykes Hall. He

strongly suspected that it was the two sons of Ambrose Carleton who were to blame. He accordingly caught and imprisoned in Carlisle Castle John Carleton; his accomplices having fled, as was customary on these occasions, into Scotland.

Equally active among those whom Scrope called "the Inglish disobedients" were the inhabitants of Bewcastle and Gilsland and the surrounding districts, such as Willeva and Spadeadam Waste. It was in 1572 that some of the inhabitants of these parts, mainly Carricks from Willeva, conceived the idea of cashing in on the confusion that followed the Rising of the North by running a foray into the dominions of the Bishop of Durham. Their objective was Weardale, and their expedition has gone down to history as the Rookhope Ryde.

It was by no means the first time that the Durham men had been assailed in this fashion.

> For great troubles they've had in hand,
> With Borderers pricking hither and thither,
> But the greatest fray that e'er they had
> Was with the men of Thirlwall and Williehaver.

The reivers, however, seem to have reckoned without their hosts, the Rookhope men; whose ballad of victory goes on:

> And such a storm amongst them fell
> As I think you never heard the like;
> For he that bears his head so high,
> He oft-times falls into the dyke.

The Cumberland men, in fact, were ignominiously defeated, but the loss of some of their number in the battle, together with the six hundred sheep they had rounded up, was not the only misfortune they suffered; for on their return journey they found Haydon Bridge chained against them, as was the custom when it was known that a rode was in progress, and they were forced to ford the South Tyne before they could return to base.

Along the upper reaches of the Black and White Lyne (or Leven as the rivers used to be known) lived the English Nixons, including at one time the villainous Cuddie (Cuthbert) Nixon, more usually known as Blanketlugs. Further east were the Nobles, who produced the famous Hobbie Noble, while to the west of the Routledges dwelt the Taylors and Hetheringtons, all of them active in what they no doubt considered a good cause.

Over the Border, along the lower reaches of Liddel Water, resided the main body of the Armstrongs. One of the largest surnames of all, they could muster in their heyday more than three thousand horsemen. As time went on, however, and more and more were put to the horn, they began to appear in the Debatable Lands and, like many of the Nixons and Bells, on the English side of the Border.

In the end the surname virtually ceased to function as such; separate graynes and individuals carrying on the reiving tradition as best they could. And very successful they were; though the mere fact of their dispersal eventually debased them to a miscellaneous collection of horse and cattle thieves.

At the height of their power, the Armstrongs probably succeeded in plundering the English countryside more effectively than any other clan. "They lie still never a night," sighed one of the Wardens of the West March. What is more, they had an unpleasant habit (from the warden's point of view) of intermarrying with English surnames, and enlisting their aid in the forays that they ran into Cumberland and Tynedale.

Traditionally the chief of the Armstrongs was the laird of Mangerton, and successive hedesmen were among the foremost reivers of their day. Yet, judging from the number of times that they feature in official correspondence, it was the lairds of Whithaugh and their grayne who caused more trouble still, with Lance Armstrong and his son, Sim of the Cathills, robbing and burning their way merrily through the north of England.

Further up Liddel Water lay the towers of the Elliots, Croziers and Scottish Nixons, together with a few Kers, Hendersons and lesser breeds without the law. These, together with the Armstrongs themselves, were widely known as 'the limmer* thieves of Liddesdale'. Limmer thieves, of course, were not unknown in the Borders: far from it. The difference was that, whereas in other valleys it was only a proportion of the inhabitants who went in for reiving, and then either for the pot or just for devilment, in Liddesdale it was not only a business but one in which virtually every able-bodied man was a shareholder.

This, "the most offensive country against the West and Middle Marches", deserves as such to be described in some detail. Even now the wide valley of the Liddel presents a somewhat forbidding aspect. In the days of the reivers it must have been

* Scoundrel(ly).

grim indeed; a valley dotted with robber towers, shut in by bleak fells and consisting largely of quaking morass and primeval forests, of which only the tree-stumps and riverside woods now remain. So isolated was the area that the inhabitants talked of anyone outside the 'swires', or passes, which connected it with the outside world, as foreigners. It was not, for instance, till well into the nineteenth century that the valley boasted a single road, while travellers found that "through these deep and broken bogs we must *crawl*, to the great fatigue of ourselves, but the much greater injury of our horses".

Chief among these bogs was the infamous Tarras Moss, to which the Armstrongs were wont to resort in time of trouble, or at any rate to the forest lands within. This "desolate and horrible marsh", as Sir Walter Scott described it, is now largely denuded of trees, but remains a pretty gloomy place, accessible only by a narrow moorland road obstructed by half-a-dozen gates. Through it flows the Tarras Burn which, when in flood, is reputed to run with such speed that it is impossible to drown in it "for, e'er the head can win down the harns* are out".

Over the wilderness of Liddesdale there still broods the lowering mass of Hermitage Castle, the scene of all kinds of medieval horror, where Sir Alexander Ramsay was left to starve to death in the dungeon, and the Wicked Lord de Soulis weaved his wizard spells. Here, in this stark and gloomy pile that seems to reflect all the cruelty and horror of Border warfare, dwelt the Keepers of Liddesdale, and here it was that Mary Queen of Scots came to visit the wounded Bothwell.

While it was in the royal fortress of Hermitage that the keepers were stationed, it was at the Redheugh that their deputies normally dwelt, for this office was the perquisite of the Elliots, or rather of their hedesman, later known as Elliot of Larriston. One of the great surnames of the Border, the Elliots, like the Armstrongs, were inclined to change their allegiance whenever it suited them, and history is full of their efforts to turn a dishonest penny by supporting the English. As, for instance, when three hundred Elliots and Croziers offered Sir Ralph Eure to become 'assured men'; or when Martin Elliot was caught out by his own countrymen in a plot to hand over Hermitage.

To the south of the Larriston Fells that form the western end of the Cheviot range, lies the valley of the North Tyne, of

* Brains.

which Sir Robert Bowes, in his report on the state of the Borders, wrote:

> The country of North Tynedale which is more plenished with wild and misdemeaned people, may make of men upon horseback and upon foot about six hundred. They stand most by four surnames, whereof the Charltons be the chief. And in all services or charge impressed upon that country the Charltons and such as be under their rule, be rated for the one half of that country, the Robsons for a quarter, and the Dodds and Milburns for another quarter.

Both Robsons and Dodds, and particularly the former, figure prominently in the annals of the Border but neither surname seems to have bred a leader of any eminence. It was the Robsons, of course, who had the dubious honour of providing the villain of the piece when the so-called Farnstein failed to appear at the day of truce, and became the unwitting cause of the fracas at the Redeswire. And it was Jamie Dodd of the Burnmouth, near Tarset, who was branded by the Earl of Surrey, when warden general, as "the most named thief of all others", before he hanged him out of hand.

The Milburns, though playing their full part in the reiving that was endemic to the valley, were another surname that seems to have thrown up few outstanding figures, though in the latter part of the seventeenth century they produced Barty of the Comb, a character celebrated both for his strength and swordsmanship. One morning, finding all his sheep to be missing, he set off with his close friend and neighbour, variously described as Hodge Corby and Corbit Jack (but probably one of the Robsons) to follow the tracks of the sheep down the Blakehope burn into Redesdale and over Carter Fell into Scotland. Here, in the absence of a slue-dog, they lost the trail, and, on consideration, came to the same conclusion as the Welshman, Dinas Mawr, that—

> The mountain sheep are sweeter,
> But the valley sheep are fatter;
> We therefore deemed it meeter,
> To carry off the latter.

So from Lethem, in the little valley of the Shaw Burn, Barty and his companion drove off a selection of wethers, closely followed by two Scotsmen. At Chattlehope Spout, the pursuers caught up with their quarry. They were offered half the flock if they would call it a day but, not unnaturally, refused. One of the Scots ran his sword into Barty's thigh but the wounded man, wrenching at it, broke off the blade. Corbit Jack fell dead, but Barty, forsaking the usual stroke at the thigh, took a tremendous swipe at his assailant's neck and "garred his heid spang* alang the heather like an inion". Then striking down the other Scot, he collected both swords, took his companion on his back, and drove the sheep safely home—a mere dozen miles across the fells. At least that was Barty's version of the story.

It was the Charltons who were not only the biggest surname in the valley but also the most important. Willing to turn their hand against anyone, so long as it was likely to show them a profit, they would then retire into the glens of North Tyne, such as the Lewisburn valley, which was described by those who had failed to winkle them out as "a marvellous strong ground of wood and water". When not engaged in robbery at home and in the Bishopric of Durham, it was in Scotland, of course, that the Charltons 'found their meat', as when the Governor of Berwick was informed that "the laird of Hawkhope was slain on Friday last in Jedward Forest in stealing. Ane tuik him on the heid and dang out all his harns." Their speciality, however, was to encourage others to ride, and then to lay an ambush and make off with the proceeds.

To the east of North Tyne, and running down from the Border to meet it, flows the Rede. Whereas Lord Dacre once wrote about the thieves of Tynedale that he would rather "lose one finger of every hand than to meddle therewith" another contemporary described the men of Redesdale as "even of like nature as to Tynedale men save that they be not so truly of their words and promise". "Naughty, evil, unruly and mis-demeanoured" was how a future warden was to characterize them.

So far as the Newcastle Company of Merchant Adventurers were concerned, there was nothing to choose between the two 'robber valleys', for members were forbidden to accept appren-tices from either, on pain of paying a fine of twenty pounds; a rule that, significantly, was not repealed until 1771.

Like their brethren in Tynedale, the reivers of Redesdale

* Bound.

made themselves particularly unpopular with the Warden of
the Middle March not only by plundering their own compatriots but by aiding and abetting their counterparts in Liddesdale in doing the same. It was in 1559, for instance, that they
were involved in the kind of escapade that must have made
the enforcement of the Border Laws something of a nightmare.
With the willing assistance of the Redesdale men, a party of
reivers from Liddesdale 'took up' Sweethope, some miles east
of Bellingham; the plan being for the two contingents to divide,
once the fray was over; the prisoners being escorted back
through North Tynedale, while the cattle were driven up the
valley of the Rede. Here it was, at Cottonshope, that a party
of Tynedale men, riding a foray into Scotland, came upon the
cattle and made off with them while their captors were baiting
their horses. It was some time before the latter could find a
slue-dog and follow the trod into the recesses of Tynedale
where, unfortunately, the story ends.

Almost parallel to the valleys of the Rede and North Tyne,
and only separated from Scotland by the Cheviot heights, lies
Coquetdale whose inhabitants were reckoned to be the "best
prepared for defence and most defensible people of themselves. And of the truest and best sort of any that do inhabit
endlong all the frontier or border of the said Middle March of
England." The best prepared for defence they may have been,
but life must have been anything but easy for them, for not
only did they have to contend with reivers from Teviotdale
but also with their own countrymen from Redesdale and North
Tyne.

Nevertheless it was from the valleys of the upper Teviot and
Borthwick Water, west of Hawick, that they had most to fear.
Here lived the Rutherfords, Turnbulls, Burns and, above all, the
Scotts of Branxholm, Gilmanscleuch, Harden, Goldielands and
others who, when not engaged in deadly feud with the Elliots
or Kers, sought their profit over the Border under the overall
leadership of the lairds of Buccleuch, with their headquarters
at Branxholm.

Vying with the Scotts for supremacy of the Middle March
stood the Kers. What is now known as the Lothian branch
operated from the lands around Ferniehirst Castle, just south
of Jedburgh, while the Roxburghe grayne centred around Cessford, rather further to the east. Irritable and capricious by

nature, the Kers seem to have been blood-thirsty and arrogant even above their fellows. Whether their leaders were bidding against each other for the wardenship of the Middle March, feuding with their neighbours or crossing the Border to fire the 'towns' of Northumberland, they remained an enigma which neither government succeeded in solving. At one moment they would be loyal, charming servants of their king: the next they would be unpredictable bandits. Ferniehirst alone, according to Sir Ralph Sadler when he was ambassador to the Scottish court, could command more than three thousand men.

From the same spy who gave Sadler the information about Ferniehirst came details of the standing that the Homes enjoyed in the East March, the wardenship of which was hereditary to the family. Chief among them, of course, were the Lords Home, who spent some of their time at Home Castle, but more in Edinburgh and elsewhere. Running them very close in influence, however, were the Lairds of Wedderburn and of Coldenknowes, so that between them the Homes formed an oligarchy that, for all practical purposes, ruled the Lothians and the Merse, when they were not engaged in quarrelling among themselves.

When it came to quarrelling and brawling, however, it was the Northumberland gentry, and certain families in particular, who seem to have taken the palm. On occasion they could be persuaded to unite against the common enemy but, as soon as the danger was over (as when Flodden had been fought and won) they would be at each other's throats once more. Selbys murdered Reaveleys, Horsleys murdered Claverings and Carrs, while Turpins, Pawstons and Rutherfords were arraigned for "slaughter done and [significantly] not agreed for".

Like the gentry of Cumberland, when not themselves engaged in violence, they were perfectly prepared to encourage others in their reiving, even when they themselves occupied positions of trust. The Duke of Norfolk, when given command against the Scots, was one of those who complained not only of the chaotic conditions in Northumberland but of the fact that those who should have known better were "looking through their fingers" at what went on. Lord Hunsdon, when he was Warden of the Middle March, was to go even further and accuse the officials in South Tyne of actually aiding the Liddesdale men. Messrs. Ridley and Heron, he said, had taken little or no action to prevent the Scots from burning Haydon Bridge. "I have very vehement suspicions," he went on, "that Ridley himself and some other Englishmen have been acquainted and the drawers of the Scots to Haydon Bridge—which, if I find true, I will make them hop headless, whosoever they be".

CHAPTER NINE

Tactics. The Hot Trod

Nae bastles or peels
Are safe frae the de'ils
Gin the collies be oot, or the laird's awae.
The bit bairnies and wives
Gang i' dread o' their lives,
For they scumfish them oot wi' the smoutherin' strae.

J. Crawhall, 'The Hot Trod'

No-one has described more clearly than Bishop Leslie how the reivers set about their work. "They sally out of their own borders in troops," he wrote,

> through unfrequented ways and many intricate windings. In the day time they refresh themselves and their horses in lurking places they had pitched on before, till they arrive in the dark at those places they have a design upon. As soon as they have seized upon their booty, they in like manner return home in the night; through blind ways and fetching many a compass. The more skilful any captain is to pass through these wild deserts, and crooked turnings and deep precipices, in the thickest mist and darkness, his reputation is the greater, and he is looked upon as a man of an excellent head, and they are so very cunning that they seldom have their booty taken from them, unless sometimes, when by the help of bloodhounds, following them exactly upon the track, they may chance to fall into the hands of their adversaries. When being taken they have so much persuasive eloquence, and so many smooth and insinuating words at command, that if they do not move their judges, nay and even their adversaries, to have mercy, yet they incite them to admiration and compassion.

The first essential in running such a foray was a place of rendezvous where the participants might collect. Every grayne, in fact, had a designated spot, known to all its members and often marked by a cairn of stones on the open moor, such as Bewcastle Dale and Spadeadam Waste. Here, latecomers would find a mark cut in the turf, or the bark of a tree, showing the direction in which the raiding party had gone. In Linton (Roxburghshire) in Sir Walter Scott's day, there was still to be seen a circle of stones surrounding an area of smooth turf, and known as the tryst, where it had been the practice to cut in the grass the name of the leader of the expedition; the direction of travel being shown by the extension, as it were, of the name.

At such places the members of the raiding party would assemble with their arms and rations, though apparently nothing in the way of shelter from the rigours of a night spent in the open. If a hedesman was present he would carry a trumpet, but banners were unusual except in time of war. Dr Magnus, for instance, when English Resident at the court of Scotland, found it an occasion for official complaint that the Borderers were riding in great numbers with banners displayed; a sure sign of mischief.

After the men themselves, the most important factor in any foray was, of course, the quality of the mounts on which, as has already been suggested, their very lives depended. So long as a reiver owned a speedy horse, he was 'not mickle careful for the rest of the household gear'.

Perhaps it was not every reiver who, like "Watt Tinlinn from the Liddelside",

> . . . led a small and shaggy nag,
> That, through a bog, from hag to hag,
> Could bound like any Billhope stag.

Nevertheless there is no doubt about the ability of "the sagacious galloway" to pick his way among the bogs and stagnant pools, and find by instinct the only safe passage.

Speed, staying power and the ability to find a way through the mosses were not, however, the only virtues that a reiver required of his horse. The animal, like its rider, must be able to drive back the motley collections of cattle, sheep, horses and even pigs and goats that had been lifted. The reiver, in fact, must be an expert cowhand, and his pony equally adept.

Off would go the raiders then, as Leslie says, in broad daylight; jack on back, steel cap on head, bow, lance or Jeddart axe in hand, and little shaggy pony underneath. When they reached their destination, it would be their aim to lift what livestock they could during the hours of darkness and in such a way as to avoid bloodshed and delay any retribution for as long as possible.

If, however, for reasons of revenge or because of a need for insight, it was necessary to attack the victim's tower, the question would arise how best to set about the task. The easiest way to reduce the place would be by cannon fire but, even in the case of a warden rode, this was rarely practicable, owing to the difficulty of dragging artillery over the Border fells and mosses. For reivers its use was, of course, out of the question. Gunpowder might come in handy if one wanted to destroy a building already gutted of its contents or deserted by its occupants, but any such approach to the problem could easily be foiled if the owner liked to fill his tower with peat and leave it to smoulder, in which case it would be suicidal for anyone to try and blow it up.

Sir Ralph Eure, after his expedition into Scotland with Sir Brian Layton, reported that they "went to a town of the Lord Buccleuch, called Mosshouse, and won the Barmkin, and gat many nags and nolt and smoked very sore the tower and took thirty prisoners". This involved hewing down the barmkin gate with axes, and then 'scumfishing'* the inhabitants of the tower by heaping damp straw against the walls and setting fire to it. The same technique could also be applied even more easily to the caves along the banks of Teviot and Jed Water where the reivers hid their ill-gotten gains.

Before scumfishing the inhabitants of a tower, however, it might be necessary first to 'wicker' the door by piling brushwood against it: then to burn it down and wrench open the iron yett with crowbars. Alternatively, the tower might be scaled with ladders; a method which, one would have thought, was highly dangerous to the attackers, but was nevertheless a favourite of Sir Robert Carey, who describes in his memoirs how he collected a number of the Carlisle townsmen, "whom we presently set to work, to get to the top of the tower and to uncover the roof; and then some twenty of them to fall down together and by that means to win the tower".

Perhaps the best method of all on the rare occasions when

* Suffocating, smoking out.

circumstances permitted, was by stealth; as when Carleton, during his lengthy inroad into Dumfriesshire, wished to seize the Lochwood in the absence of Lord Johnstone. Sending a party into the barmkin before dawn, he captured the two watchmen; then waited until a serving wench opened the iron yett of the tower. Seeing the intruders, she hastily withdrew; "but one got hold of it that she could not get it close to . . . and she being troubled with the wood door left the iron door open and so we entered and won the Lochwood".

Reiving, luckily for those who had to suffer its effects, was largely a seasonal occupation. Sir Robert Carey reported that the

Borderers will never lightly steal hard before Lammas* . . . unless in such years as they cannot ride upon the wastes by reasons of storms and snows, the last months of the year are their chief time for stealing, for then are the nights longest, their horses hard at meat and will ride best, cattle strong and will drive furthest. After Candlemas† the nights grow short, and cattle grow weaker, and oats growing dearer, they feed their horses worse and quickly turn them to grass.

A certain amount of reiving persisted into the spring and even, on occasion, into early summer, but more for purposes of revenge than for the pot. Not only were the nights too short to give the reivers a reasonable start on their pursuers or, for the matter of that, to make their final approach in secrecy, but there would be little flesh on the cattle, for until the introduction of turnips in the eighteenth century the number of animals that could be carried through the winter was strictly limited, and those that had survived on a diet of straw and a little hay would certainly be in no condition for slaughter.

Livestock, however, though the easiest to lift, were not the only plunder to attract the reiver. While any form of insight was plainly grist to his mill, he would not be averse to collecting, in addition, as much grain as he could carry. It was for this reason and because, as a farmer himself, he would not be free to ride while busy with his own harvest, that the close season was more likely to extend beyond Lammas.

* 1st August.
† 2nd February.

What was sauce for the reiver was also sauce for the warden, if he wanted to strike when it hurt most. Thomas, Lord Dacre, for example, once wrote to the Earl of Surrey that he proposed to delay a raid into Scotland until Michaelmas, when the offenders' corn would have been cut, and "they will be utterly ruined".

Even to the experienced reiver, a dark October night could present problems when he had to pick his way over bog and fell with little but his own memory and his horse's instinct to help him. Moonlight, therefore, assumed the utmost importance. Even the normally prosaic Pitcairn, in his *Criminal Trials of Scotland*, so far forgot himself as to write of the Olivers "making the most of the recent Michaelmas moon, the Goddess of the Borders". But perhaps the most notable instance of the value that the reivers placed on moonlight is to be found in a tradition associated with that Walter Scott, who was known to history as Wat o' Harden. He was married to Mary Scott, known because of her beauty as the Flower of Yarrow, and between them they produced a daughter who was in turn nick-named, because of her resourceful, managing nature, Maggie Fendy. She it was who married Gilbert Elliot of Stobs, known far and wide as Gibbie o' the Gowden Garters. The marriage settlement is alleged to have consisted, in part, of a contract whereby the couple were to be allowed to stay as guests of Old Wat in his tower at Dryhope for a year and a day. In return Gibbie was to hand over to his father-in-law the *plunder of the first harvest moon*.

The extent to which the 'riding families' chose to operate in what Lord Dacre called "the pride of the moon", and the importance of the stars in affording them guidance, are reflected by the frequency with which one or the other appeared in mottoes, and on coats of arms. The shield of the Scotts of Buccleuch, for instance, bore a star and two crescent moons, and either "Best riding by moonlight" or *"Luna cornua reparabit"*, meaning that the moon would replenish their coffers. Variations used by some of the Scotts were a shield with two stars and a single crescent, and mottoes such as "We'll have moonlight again".

Another motto of the Scotts was "Watch weel"; of the Johnstones "Aye ready" and the Douglases "Forward". The Dicksons varied "I sleep but watch" with "Fortune favours the

(*above*) Askerton Castle, the official residence of Thomas Carleton and other land sergeants. (*below*) The scrubby land bordering the Tarset Burn at the Comb, to which Barty Milburn brought back the sheep from Lethem.

(*above*) "Maxwell reached the Annan . . . and so began the battle of Dryfe Sands." (*below*) "To the east of North Tyne, and running down from the Border to meet it, flows the Rede."

bold", while "Spare nought" was the uncompromising maxim of the Hays of Tweeddale.

Proudest and most typical of the Border mottoes were the Cranstouns', "Thou shalt want ere I want", and the Elliots' "Wha daur meddle wi' me", which reflect all the bumptious arrogance of the reiver. For five hundred years the Elliots' boast has fascinated those who have encountered it. Buccleuch's trumpets are supposed to have sounded the call in triumph at the liberation of Kinmont Willie, and a ballad put into the mouth of Little Jock Elliot (the supposed conqueror, but actually the victim, of the fourth Earl of Bothwell) uses it as a refrain.

> I vanquished the Queen's lieutenant,
> And gar'd his fierce troopers flee,
> My name is little Jock Elliot,
> And wha daur meddle wi' me?
>
> I ride on my fleet-footed gray,
> My sword hanging down by my knee,
> I ne'er was afraid of a foe,
> And wha daur meddle wi' me?

Every grayne had its own slogan which, serving both as battle cry and watchword, was particularly useful in the dark. In Scotland this usually echoed the name of the rendezvous. Thus the Cranstouns were wont to shout "Henwoodie" (from their gathering ground on Oxnam Water), and the Maxwells "Wardlaw, Wardlaw, I bid you bide Wardlaw" (from a hill near Caerlaverock). The Hallidays, however, often used their clan name, "A Holy day, a Holy day", and the Homes "A Home, a Home" in the same way as the Borderers on the English side, who shouted "A Shafto, a Shafto" or "a Fenwick, a Fenwick". Sometimes a group slogan might be employed, such as those that enlivened the fray at the Redeswire, or the cry of the men of North Tyne when on mischief bent,

> Tarset Burn and Tarret Burn,
> Hard and heather bred.
> Yet, Yet, Yet,

which simply meant 'Make way there'.

Another alternative was to use the crest as a slogan; the Dacres, for instance, shouting "A Read* Bull, a Read Bull".

* Red.

When the Scots, at Flodden, "charged in good order after the Almayns* manner without speaking a word", it came as quite a surprise to the onlookers, for ordinarily "the slogan's deadly yell" of the Borderers, Scots and English alike, was enough to curdle the blood. At any rate this was the opinion of 'inland men' like Patten, who described the Borderers in battle as "not unlike (to be plain) unto a masterless hound howling in a highway, when he hath lost him he waited upon, some hooping, some whistling, and most with crying "a Berwick! a Berwick! a Fenwick! a Fenwick! a Bulmer! a Bulmer!" In the same passage, Patten explained that these were rallying cries to keep the clans together in battle, but commented that if every man used them, the result would be "more like the outrage of a dissolute hunting, than the quiet of a well-ordered army".

"In Tynedale,† where I was born," wrote Bishop Ridley, "I have known my countrymen watch night and day in their harness, such as they had, that is in their jacks, and their spears in their hands (you call them northern gads). . . . And so doing, although at every such bickerings some of them spent their lives, yet by such means, like pretty men, they defended their country".

The constant state of vigilance required of these pretty men involved the keeping of Watch and Ward; in other words, a state of wakefulness by night, and looking out in a specified direction by day. The Border Laws of England, in particular, laid down in detail which places should be guarded; how and by whom; the particulars appearing in the

Orders of the Marches upon the West, Middle and East Marches made by Lord Wharton, Lord Deputy General of all the three Marches, under my Lord of Northumberland's Grace, Lord Warden of all the said Marches, in the month of October in the sixth year of the reign of our Sovereign Lord, King Edward VI.

These orders laid down that ward should be kept by day from the hills that commanded a view of the tracks and 'passages' which the reivers were likely to use, and watch by night on the passes, and particularly on the fords. Strangers were to

* German.
† The old tower is still to be seen at Willimoteswick, near Haltwhistle.

be challenged and, if no proper explanation was forthcoming, "taken before Baylifs and Constables to be tryed". The watches were to be kept from 1st October to 16th March; the night watch "to be set on the day-going, and to continue unto the day be light; and the day watch, where the same is, to begin at the daylight and to continue unto the day be gone".

The regulations specified with great exactitude not only the passes and fords to be watched and the 'towns' responsible for each, but the officials who would ensure that this responsibility was properly carried out. These were the setters, or gentlemen of the district who actually posted the watches, and the searchers who would visit them at intervals to see if they were awake. Over all were the land sergeants, bailiffs and other officers who would report to the warden on the general efficiency of the system.

Further orders were made as required, such as the rule that the warden should be informed immediately of any deaths among those eligible for watch-keeping. Within the general regulations there were also more localized ones. "The tenants of Ferneley," for instance, were ordered to "keep a watchman about the houses" and the Coquetdale men to keep a night watch against their neighbours in Redesdale. So dangerous, and so brazen, did the Scottish reivers and their allies, the Grahams and 'broken men', become that, in peace as in war, sentinels manned the walls of Carlisle day and night; the gates being, of course, shut at dusk, and "a chain drawn up between the city and the head of the Eden bridges".

When the authorities suspected that the reivers were about to run a large-scale foray, they might post a 'plump', or outsize watch of anything up to forty men. Normally, however, there would only be two on watch at any given time. It must have been an unenviable task. Every rustle, every unusual murmur of the water beside which they were posted, might signal the approach of an enemy brought up, like a Red Indian, to make the minimum of noise. If a watcher heard nothing, he might still feel that his throat would be cut before he could see what was behind him. If he did hear something, it might or might not turn out to be the searcher checking that he was awake. Though it was his duty to get word back to his fellows as soon as he knew an enemy to be approaching, there was always the possibility that by so doing he would raise a false alarm. He must therefore challenge first and, if the answer revealed an enemy, he would have to choose between fighting, in which case he stood a good chance of being felled and then chopped in pieces, or departing quickly to raise the alarm, and risk being charged with March Treason for not engaging the enemy.

The system of organized watch and ward was not, of course, enough in itself to provide protection for the population. A man must be ready at all times to defend himself. Thus, when workmen repaired Norham Castle, they were instructed to wear not only steel caps or sallets, but jacks as well. Shepherds were quite accustomed to watch their flocks, pike in hand, and a Frenchman, Dr Perlin, reported that "the people are all armed and the labourers, when they till the ground, leave their swords and their bows in a corner of the field".

Where the terrain was suitable, it was simple enough, if decidedly inconvenient, for the Borderers to retire, on the reivers' approach, to the mosses and forests, if not into the peels provided for the purpose. Nevertheless, if only to prevent the lifting of livestock, the authorities were always looking for ways and means of making forays more difficult of execution. It was Lord Wharton, once more, whose idea it was that "portions of land convenient for tillage, meadows or grazing, should be enclosed in ditches five quarters in breadth, six in depth, double set with quickwood and hedged about three quarters high", and that the necessary quicksets should be sold in the churches. Narrow passes, moreover, were to be blocked, and fords "stopped and destroyed". In practice fords were actually dammed up, while those across the Tweed were planted with willows. Finally, "a dyke of force", that was to provide a model for the Scottish Dyke dividing the Debatable Lands, was cut from the junction of the Redden Burn with the Tweed all the way to Harbottle.

A vital part of the early warning system was the network of beacons spread out over the countryside. In the West March of England, for instance, it extended all the way south from Spadeadam Waste across the peaks of the Lake District to Barbon in North Lancashire. Control of these networks was chiefly exercised from Carlisle Castle on the English, and Home Castle on the Scottish, side. It was the watchman at Home who, in 1804, mistook the fires of charcoal burners near Berwick for beacons heralding the approach of Napoleon's invasion army and, by his example, set off all the other Border beacons, thus causing the volunteers to fly to arms.

Originally, the beacons, known as 'bales' from the Old English word for a funeral fire, or 'need fires' after those produced by rubbing two sticks together, were just piles of logs. These were located on hillsides preferably six to seven hundred feet high, and easy of access for the horse and cart of the watchman, who was supposed to be in permanent readiness. In the course of time, however, beacons became more sophisticated. Scottish regulations of the fifteenth century, for example, prescribed that they should take the form of "a long and strong tree, set up with a long iron pole across the head of it, and an iron brander* fixed on a stalk in the middle of it for holding a tar barrel".

Hill beacons were gradually supplemented by grates held in heavy stone lanterns on the roof of every tower and castle. Regulations on the English side laid down that "Everie man that hath a castle or tower of stone shall upon every fray raised in the night give warning to the countrie by fire on the topps of the castle tower in such sort as he shall be directed from the warning castle upon paine of 3/4d".

In Scotland, later instructions took much the same form, and were all the more effective because the lie of the land allowed towers to be built every two or three miles, which made the passing of warnings comparatively easy. Not only must every tower have on it an iron basket to hold the bale, but a regular code of signals was developed, from which the speed and strength of an attack from the English side could be communicated. "One bale is warning of their coming, what power that even they be of: two bales together at once, they are coming indeed: four bales, each one beside other, and all at once as four candles, sure knowledge that they are of great power".

There were special regulations, also, governing the use of beacons on towers occupied by Border officials. At Hoddam, in Dumfriesshire, for instance, "Ane wise stout man" must ensure that the bale was kept burning so long as an Englishman remained in Scotland, and a bell rung whenever an enemy hove in sight. The regulations for the Barony of Gilsland required

* Conical grid.

the victim of a foray to keep a fire burning "on some height" so that "all men may know which way to draw".

Nowhere does there seem to have been any provision for an 'All Clear', except perhaps at Hoddam, where the wise stout man must have been hard put to it to know when the last Englishman had finished desecrating Scottish soil. It is to be presumed, therefore, that when the original supply of fuel was exhausted nothing further would be added. Otherwise there would be no knowing when the raid was over. Again, how far afield should the bales be lit? If it were only a couple of reivers running a minor foray, must every beacon be kindled from the Solway all the way to Edinburgh?

Beacons, of course, were mainly used at night, though the black smoke from a bale might send its message a fair distance in daylight. In Liddesdale it was the custom for white sheets to be spread on convenient bushes. In addition, there would be bells to ring, as at Hoddam. At Hexham there hung a Fray Bell which, when it was broken up in 1742, was found to weigh some three tons. This was used to signal the appearance of reivers not only from Scotland but from neighbouring Tynedale and Redesdale. Perhaps it is not too late to point out that a 'fray' denoted any kind of disturbance, and particularly an armed one; as distinct from a 'foray', which was the expedition that might, or might not, develop into a fray.

It is worth trying to picture the scene, once the alarm has been given. From hill to hill, and tower to tower, all over the fells there will be lights winking like glow-worms in a hedge-side. It may be that the alarm has been raised in time, and the neighbours, rushing to arms as soon as they see the beacons and hear the commotion, will be able to meet, and possibly to repulse, the raiders. It is even more likely that the robbery will have been carried out by stealth and that all that remains for the victims is to 'follow their goods'. From every tower, farm and cottage will come the men who have worked and slept with their weapons beside them. Armed and horsed, they carry flaming on the points of their lances the signal which will proclaim to all and sundry the pursuit in which they are legally bound to join.

Though usually known as the 'wisp', or 'burning strae', this is unlikely to be of straw and will more probably consist of a smouldering divot of peat snatched from the fire and fanned to flame by the speed of the chase. The rallying point will be at the traditional rendezvous and, as soon as a posse is assembled, off they will gallop after the raiders. For this is the 'hot trod', and the pursuers, in the words of Sir Robert Bowes, "may lawfully follow their goods either with a sleuth hound the trod* thereof, or else by such other means as they best can devise". The Border laws, in fact, made specific allowance for "parties grieved to follow their lawful trod with hound and horn, with hue and cry, and all other manner of fresh pursuit, for the recovery of their goods spoiled"; no safe-conduct being required if it proved necessary to cross the Border.

Originally, no safe-conduct had been required of "a man following his goods with hound or without horn, or with both without spear or bow" when crossing the Border. Subsequent regulations, however, allowed him to do so fully armed, but required him to "go to any man of good fame and sound judgment and, declaring his cause", specify what the goods were and ask the person concerned to "witness the trod". It cannot have been easy to find a "man of good fame" in those parts and the rule was eventually relaxed to allow the pursuer to inform instead the first 'town', or first person he met, of the reason for his coming. He was still entitled, however, to ask for assistance in his just pursuit.

These instructions applied to wardens as much as to anyone else, though they were often ignored. If a pursuing warden were hindered in any way when following the hot trod, the offender was to be punished. On the other hand, if the warden or one of his men caused any injury or harm considered to be unlawful in this context, he was to be handed over to the opposite warden. An example of such an offence is to be found in a raid on Tynedale by "the Bold Buccleuch" when Keeper of Liddesdale; the English complaining to James VI that the Keeper had slaughtered a number of men other than "thieves taken with the red hand", and had "forfeited his trod" by going out of his way to burn as well as arrest.

In 1570 the punishment for failing to follow the fray was reduced to seven days' imprisonment or a fine of 3s 4d; a welcome substitute for the death penalty that had previously been applied. Even then, there were local by-laws such as that of the manor of Embleton, which imposed a fine of 6s 8d on any

* Track.

horsemen who failed to "give their attendance of the bailiff and other officer to be ready to go with the dog altogether".

On the other hand, there were certain rewards to be won by those who followed the trod, such as the "rescue shot" which was paid by Jamie Telfer, in the ballad of that name, "baith wi' gowd and white monie". According to the tariff published by the Council of the North, those on the English side of the Border were to be paid one shilling in the pound on all cattle that they helped to recover in their own country, and two shillings if in Scotland.

If, for one reason or another, the hot trod was impracticable, there remained other methods of reclaiming one's goods. One possibility was to appeal within six days of the loss to the warden, who would then take the matter up with his counterpart. Another was to apply to the opposite warden for a safe conduct that would give the injured party enough time to take back what belonged to him by force. A third alternative was the 'cold trod', which did not, according to the Border laws, require a safe conduct so long as it was followed within six days, and "the first honest man inhabiting within the Marches which he hath entered" witnessed the pursuit.

The fact that it was illegal for anyone to obstruct a pursuer on his 'lawful trod' did little or nothing to reduce the risk of being ambushed by the guilty parties, or by any other ill-disposed person. It was in 1580, for instance, that a number of English reivers stole some cattle from the Gladstones in Liddesdale. The latter pursued them into Cumberland as far as Billieheid (Baileyhead) where they 'rypit for the nowt'—that is to say, searched for the cattle—but without success. Then, to add insult to injury, they fell into the hands of that notorious scoundrel, Lancie Armstrong, the laird of Whithaugh. Probably the latter was just hovering like a vulture to alight on any carrion that might come his way. If so, he must have been disappointed to find no booty.

All was not in vain, however, for as well as one of the Gladstones being killed and another dozen wounded, no less than forty were taken prisoner and forced 'to make band and promise to Whithaugh', which meant that they must come to the assistance of these particular Armstrongs within eight days of being summoned. It is typical of the honour among thieves that obtained in this strange, twilight world of robbery and violence that, despite the fact that the Whithaugh grayne had been denounced as rebels, put to the horn, and their goods confiscated, no-one would have doubted for a moment that such a promise would be kept.

Two years after this, Humfrey Musgrave was following the hot trod against some Scottish reivers, when the pursued, with that lightning rapidity that strangers to the Border found so disconcerting, rallied their neighbours and turned on their pursuers, who were accordingly forced to retreat. Rather than return with nothing, Musgrave, as seems to have been customary in this Border game of musical chairs, seized the nearest chair he could find, in the shape of some sheep and nolt* belonging to another Scotsman.

It is no accident that in accounts of the hot trod there are so many references to 'going with the dog', 'hound and horn', and so forth. Reivers driving what was often a motley collection of animals were able to make very little speed, particularly if pigs formed part of their booty. Given that they had not too much start, therefore, it would not be difficult to catch them up so long as one could follow their tracks. Without a dog, however, this was usually a forlorn hope. The hounds which were, in fact, used to follow the trail were probably the ancestors not so much of the modern bloodhound as of the trailhounds still so popular in Cumberland and elsewhere, and of the foxhounds still in use in the Borders. Perhaps it was some of their descendants whom a huntsman of the Mellerstain with difficulty prevented from running down a woman when they were ostensibly concentrating on a fox.

These hounds, which were kept at stipulated places within the Marches, were sometimes known as 'lurg dogs' (perhaps because of the length of their ears rather than their being lugged on a thong) but more often as 'slue', or sleuth, dogs on account of their ability to follow a slot or trail. Without their assistance it would have been next to impossible to pick up the trod or, having done so, to find a way through the mosses by night. It is not surprising, therefore, that anyone who obstructed a slue-dog in the course of its duty 'shall be holden as accessarie unto the theft'. Possibly he should have considered himself lucky that the punishment was not made to fit the crime, as in the

* Neat, or cattle.

case of an earlier law in Scotland. This laid down that "if any man slays another man's hound, he shall watch upon that man's midden for a twelvemonth and a day or shall answer him of all his skaiths* that him shall fall . . . for fault of his watch hound".

There were two possible defences against the slue-dog. The first was for the reivers to slaughter one of the animals they were herding, in the hope that the hound would stop to devour what it could of the carcase. If this ploy failed, they must imitate that "stark, moss-trooping" Scott, William of Deloraine, in the *Lay of the Last Minstrel*, who

> By wily turns, by desperate bounds,
> Had baffled Percy's best blood-hounds.

This he would endeavour to do by riding down convenient rivers and burns, in order to destroy the scent.

So valuable were slue-dogs as an insurance against permanent loss that the dogs themselves were often to be found among the spoils of a foray, and a really good one could change hands for the relatively enormous price of £25 sterling. Their importance is further shown by the regulations of the Barony of Gilsland which included a requirement for every tenant to keep a hound; and by the 'calendar' which the English wardens kept, showing exactly where every slue-dog in their wardenry was to be found. Nor did the necessity to track down cattle thieves disappear with the Union of the crowns, for in 1616 the Commissioners still found it necessary to stipulate that hounds be kept at stipulated places in Cumberland; namely "Foot of Sark, Moat within Sark, the Bailie Head near Arthuret, Tinkler Hall, Stapleton, Irthington, Lanercost, Kirklington and Rawcliffe".

* Damages, hurts.

CHAPTER TEN

Deadly Feud

And at the sacred fount, the priest
Through ages left the master hand unblest,
To urge with keener aim, the blood-encrusted spear.
John Leyden

It is difficult to read (or, for the matter of that, to write) much about the Border without coming across what James VI described as "the auld and detestable monster of deadly feid".

Deadly feud, or 'feid' as it was usually spelt, seems to have been a fairly common disease throughout Scotland and the extreme north of England. It would be profitless to enquire too closely into its origin, except to point out that the Early English never demanded a life for a life, but recognized instead a 'blood-wyt' which laid down the compensation payable for the slaughter of different classes of person; a concept which to some extent, persisted in the Border Laws. The circumstances of the time, however, together with the difficulty of obtaining proper justice in the Borders had led to a reversion to the biblical (and possibly the Celtic) law of 'eye for eye and tooth for tooth'.

If a man was slain, in whatever circumstances, it became the bounden duty of his nearest relative to avenge him; a duty that was handed down from father to son. There was therefore no obvious reason why the feud, thus created, should not persist for ever; with retaliation answering retaliation. Worse still, the duty was shared by the rest of the grayne, so that no man defending his life or property, no official who, in the course of his occupation caused someone's death; no juryman who found a person guilty on a capital charge, could count himself safe from revenge on himself, his family or grayne.

So much did revenge became part of the Borderer's code of

honour that the Church itself was forced to recognize its importance, even it it frowned upon the spirit that inspired it. In fact it became quite normal, when baptizing a male child, for his right hand (or, perhaps a Ker's left hand) to be left unchristened so that, in the words of Sir Walter Scott, "it might deal the more deadly, in fact the more unhallowed, blow to the enemy". 'Deadly feid' had, in fact, become respectable.

One of the most famous Border feuds was between the Scotts of Buccleuch and the Kers of Cessford which, despite every effort to damp it down, smouldered on for most of the sixteenth century. It was in 1526, when James V was only fourteen and completely under the thumb of the Earl of Angus, that the Laird of Buccleuch (known locally as "Wicked Wat, and by Lord Dacre as "the chief maintenance of all misguided men on the Borders") decided that the young king must be rescued from the clutches of the Douglases. When James embarked on an expedition to "daunton the thieves of the Border", therefore, Buccleuch invited him to stay at Branxholm. Angus, however, was too old a hand to fall for such a ploy, and it became apparent that what could not be achieved by guile must be attained by force, Buccleuch, therefore, collected an army of nearly a thousand Scotts, Elliots and Armstrongs and marched to the Bridge of Melrose, where he lay in wait for Angus.

The ambush developed rapidly into a skirmish that came to be known as the Battle of Darnick. For some time, Buccleuch's supporters held their own against Angus' men, now reinforced by the Homes and Kers. As so often happened in Border warfare, the ties of marriage and of mutual ill-doing prevailed and, after a little, Buccleuch's army began to fade away, leaving their leader to escape as best he might. As the Elliot contingent made off towards Liddesdale, with the Kers in hot pursuit, Sir Andrew Ker of Cessford came up with one of the Elliots who, at a place still known as Turnagain, engaged him with his lance and killed him. As a result of his escapade, Buccleuch was forced to flee to France, but was later pardoned and returned to his estates. Elliot was not so lucky, for he was arrested and taken to Edinburgh where, "for treasonably coming against his sovereign Lord the king in proper person", as also for "common theft and reset of theft", he was duly hanged.

This was only the beginning of the feud and, over many

years, a number of dark deeds were done in the name of family honour, though none darker than that which took place a generation later in the High Street of Edinburgh. A party of Kers and their friends, including some of the Homes, came upon Wicked Wat, either by chance or design. In the ensuing fracas young Ker of Cessford seems to have held back, but Home of Coldenknowes succeeded in running Scott through the body, crying to Ker as he did so, "Strike, traitor, a stroke for thy father's sake". Perhaps it is not altogether surprising that the Scotts, after this, were unwilling to turn the other cheek.

A particularly ferocious surname were the Tweedys, whose chief was the Laird of Drumelzier, near Peebles. Tradition has it that they owed their name to the indiscretion of a female ancestor, whose husband returned after several years at the Crusades to find her dandling a bouncing boy. Blandly she explained that the child owed his origin to "the Spirit of the Tweed", who had left the river in order to father him.

The feud between this surname and the neighbouring Veitches seems to have been more than ordinarily vicious. "Wherever a Veitch and a Tweedy met," wrote a nineteenth-century Veitch, "they fought, and fought to kill". The quarrel came to a climax in 1590. The chief of the Veitches known, no doubt for excellent reasons, as the De'il o' Dawyck, had for some time spared no effort to intimidate the opposition. In this he was ably assisted by a certain Burnet, called from the name of his estate, and perhaps from his nocturnal habits, the Hoolet* of Barns.

One day, the De'il's son had occasion to ride into the town of Peebles, where opposite Neidpath Castle he found nine of the Tweedys lying in wait for him. Ambushed before and behind, he had no chance at all: "It was no fight, but bloody murder". The Veitches wasted no time in recrimination. Following John Tweedy, the young laird's guardian (and known therefore as the Tutor of Drumelzier) to Edinburgh, they laid an ambush of their own and murdered him out of hand.

One of the features of deadly feud was the effect of inter-marriage between one grayne and another, which served to spread the disease. It is not surprising, therefore, that the Tweedys' retaliation was against James Geddes, Dawyck's brother-in-law, for whom they lay in wait in the Kirk Wynd

* Owlet.

in Edinburgh and "rushit out of the said close and with shots
of pistolets slew him behind his back".

The Privy Council of Scotland endeavoured on a number of
occasions to put a stop to particular feuds. It was not until
1600, however, that an Arbitration Act was passed, which
required the parties to a quarrel to "submit to two or three
friends on either side" who should, within thirty days, meet
either to effect a reconciliation or to appoint an 'overman' who
would decide the case. Nobody seems to have taken much
notice of this and, in 1611, a Royal Proclamation referred to
the fact that "the deadly feid between Veitches and Tweedys
is as yet unreconciled", and requested the Privy Council to
call the principals together and take such measures as were
customary.

The authorities seem to have retained a touching faith that
if the parties to a feud pledged themselves not to molest each
other, their relations or friends, the Borderers' well-known
aversion to breaking a promise might ensure that peace would
result. What they never seem to have got into their heads was
that, although there might be a certain honour between thieves,
the same obligations did not extend to their common enemy,
the Government. In the case of the long drawn out feud
between the Elliots and Scotts, for instance, the assurances they
gave were flagrantly violated, and the Privy Council was moved
to demand that both surnames should show cause why they
should not "incur the pain of perjury, defamation and tarnish-
ing of perpetual honour, estimation and credit"; a clear case
of "a plague o' both your houses".

A further method of settling quarrels was to persuade the
combatants to bring their dispute before the courts. The Kers,
for example, did so in order to "pursue the slaughter of a Ker
by the Rutherfords and the Turnbulls". The object of going to
law, of course, was to agree the amount required to compen-
sate for the lives lost. The chances of success, however, were
negligible, if only because of the difficulty in proving after so
many years who was really at fault. Another alternative was
to settle the case, as it were, out of court, as when, in Northumberland, Red Martin Story agreed in return for a cash payment to forego his revenge on the Hebburns, who had caused
the death of his son John. Unfortunately, he went back on
his promise and the case had to be referred to arbitrators in

the shape of Edmund Craster and Luke Ogle. The verdict of
these gentlemen was that Story must keep his word and that
the Storys and Hebburns should be "lovers and friends as they
ought to be".

Occasionally it was possible to use what little religious feeling could be squeezed out of the protagonists to make them
mend their ways. In Pre-Reformation days, for example, one
of them might be induced to acknowledge the original fault and
make atonement by way of pilgrimage to a particular shrine;
by paying for masses for the victim's soul, or even by founding
a chantry such as that in the Kirk of St Andrew at Peebles.

A cheaper, if possibly less satisfactory, method of expiation
was for the party adjudged to be guilty to attend the parish
church in the presence of his enemy of the moment, and of
the full congregation, where he would publicly ask forgiveness
both from his Maker and from the relatives; a request, the
latter, at least, were bound to grant.

Finally, a marriage could sometimes be arranged between
representatives of the two factions. In such cases, the lady
was not entitled to the usual tocher*, but a suitable settlement
of land was made in order to provide compensation. On one
occasion an attempt was made to settle the apparently endless
feud between the graynes of Cessford and Buccleuch by a series
of marriages; but the only result seems to have been that Janet
Scott, Buccleuch's sister, married Ker of Ferniehirst, of a completely different branch of the family.

A feud, however, did not always continue non-stop. On one
occasion, Cessford and Buccleuch patched up their quarrel for
long enough to run a large-scale foray into England. Sir Cuthbert
Collingwood had lately led eight or nine hundred men into
Teviotdale in order to teach the inhabitants a lesson. The
expedition proved abortive, however, for Collingwood's intentions had been leaked to the Scots in time to give them
forty-eight hours' notice, and to present the Englishmen with
nothing but empty byres and houses. As usually happened
when enough warning was received, herds and flocks had been
driven off into the hills and forests, and insight safely hidden
away.

Teviotdale obviously could not take this incursion lying
down, and the Scotts, who had been the chief target of the

* Dowry.

raid, looked about them for allies who would join in a retali-
atory foray. The temptation was too great, and the Kers agreed
to sink their differences for the time being, and to provide a
contingent. Between them they collected no less than three
thousand men, including some from Liddesdale. When the
Scotts recruited the latter, they took care to let it be known
that their objective was the English Middle March, which they
proposed to raid on the following Thursday night. A nod was
as good as a wink to the officials of the Middle March: they
made the necessary dispositions and increased their state of
readiness. Nothing whatever happened.

Meanwhile, the Scots, using the mass of Muckle Cheviot to
mask their movements, made instead for the East March,
where they proceeded to create havoc; pausing only to detach
a party of twenty to thirty to plunder Collingwood's house
at Eslington. Here they 'took up' four or five persons. Collingwood, his two sons and four or five servants gave chase, but
the opposition was too strong, and they only just regained the
house in safety. They tried again, only to lose a number of
prisoners to the reivers, but at this point a Mr Bellasis appeared
with a body of soldiers—perhaps from the garrison at Harbottle—and engaged the Scots. In the ensuing battle fourteen
or fifteen soldiers were "moste crewelly slayne and so mangled
as they were not to be knowne who they were and so lefte
stark naked".

The main body of the Scots do not seem to have been so
successful for, despite their deception plan, Lord Hunsdon was
ready for them. Said the warden, "By the time I have hanged
forty or fifty of the prisoners, which I will do at the least, I
trust that they shall have small cause to boast of that journey".

The Kers of Cessford were by no means the only grayne
with which the Scotts of Buccleuch remained locked in deadly
feud. It was in 1564 that the Elliots, encouraged no doubt by
English money, ran a foray into Teviotdale, in the course of
which they murdered a number of people. The Scotts retaliated
in kind, and a free-for-all began which fairly shook the Border.
Official retribution was, for once, swift and positive. In the
hope of discouraging the others, five of the principal offenders
from both surnames were caught, taken to Edinburgh, tried and
beheaded by torchlight on Castle Hill. It was of no avail; for
the Elliots, cheated of their prey, returned to the attack and

(*right*) "The Charltons had captured Buccleuch and kept his sword, which they refused to give up." (*below*) "Charlton of Hesleyside would be confronted by a large dish, which, when he removed the cover, would reveal a single spur."

(*above*) Newark Tower, near Selkirk, burnt by Lord Grey of Wilton. (*left*) "A tower into which the parson might retreat and defend himself." The Vicar's Tower at Corbridge.

invaded Buccleuch's estates, burning and ravaging for ten miles around and sparing neither man, woman nor child. Buccleuch demanded of the queen permission to revenge his people; then, not waiting for a reply which he must have known would be in the negative, rode into Liddesdale, where he and his men succeeded in killing seven of the Elliots and their allies, the Croziers, and returned with as many cattle as they could drive.

The risk of becoming involved in deadly feud was something that was ever present in men's minds. So much so that, according to Sir Robert Bowes' Report on the Borders, a man "had much rather take a part of his goods again in composition than to pursue the extremity of the law". Not so the actors in that Border tragedy which was played out between the Maxwells and the Johnstones. These two great Dumfriesshire surnames; the one inhabiting Nithsdale and the other Annandale, do not seem to have troubled themselves very much about raiding into England, although bills against the Johnstones are occasionally to be found on the agenda of Border Meetings. It was the rivalry between the chiefs of the two surnames that occupied almost all their attention; a rivalry that was made ten times worse by successive kings and regents rewarding each in turn with the wardenry of the West March, to the considerable vexation of the other.

When James Douglas, Earl of Morton, was executed in 1581, John, Lord Maxwell, who had always coveted his earldom and estates, and had once been imprisoned for claiming them, was at last granted his heart's desire. Instead of remaining content with his good fortune, however, he proceeded to put the earldom at risk, preferring to use the power it gave him to enrich himself and his surname rather than make any effort to keep order. Blandly ignoring his obligations as the current warden, Maxwell (or Morton as he now was) assembled an army consisting of his own household and tenants, together with a motley collection of Armstrongs, Grahams and broken men of both countries, and set off to plunder Ettrick Forest. Here he amused himself, among other things, by capturing Adam Scott and Thomas Dalgleish and holding them in the hope of an extortionate ransome. Both of them he kept in fetters, and the unfortunate Dalgleish he chained to a tree. As a result of these activities, Morton was summoned to appear before the Privy Council to answer for his sins. Wisely, perhaps, he refused the invitation and was put to the horn, losing, of course his wardenry in the process. Predictably, a Johnstone was made warden in his place.

As a Catholic, Maxwell had never been particularly acceptable to King James; yet he seems to have returned somehow to favour. He soon quarrelled, however, with James' current favourite, the Earl of Arran, who appealed to the king for help. This was immediately forthcoming in the shape of an instruction to Johnstone of Dunskellie, the new warden, to take Maxwell into custody; and a body of troops was sent from Edinburgh to help him in his mission, only to be cut to pieces by Robert Maxwell, the chief's half-brother, at Crawfordmuir. The fat was now properly in the fire and without more ado, Robert Maxwell proceeded to burn Johnstone's castle of Lochwood, having promised to give Lady Johnstone "light enough to set on her hood".

The Maxwells then turned their attention to plunder, burning 300 houses and robbing the Johnstones of 3,000 sheep and cattle. Obedience to the king's instructions, the unfortunate Johnstone complained, had cost him 100,000 crowns. It had also triggered off a feud as fierce as anything the Border was to experience.

Obviously the Johnstones could not take their humiliation lying down, if only because of its effect on their finances, and they set out to make good their losses in the traditional Border fashion. Waiting only for the spring, they twice attacked Dumfries; but were defeated by the weather. Maxwell retaliated, and plundered the Johnstones yet again. Finally, Johnstone died—some said of a broken heart—and James was once again faced with the problem of finding a warden. Inevitably, he took what must have seemed to him the only practical course, and appointed Maxwell once more. The mind boggles at what might have happened if he had not, for neither of the two warring families were likely to tolerate an outsider. The king did, however, make it a condition that they should bury the hatchet, which ostensibly they did. But they soon dug it up again, with the Johnstones this time taking the initiative.

It was William Johnstone of Wamphray, known from his jovial nature as 'The Galliard', who re-opened the feud by attacking those staunch allies of the Maxwells, the Crichtons, who returned the compliment by catching the Galliard and hanging him on the nearest tree. Retaliation was swift and sure;

the Johnstones descending on Nithsdale like a swarm of locusts and demolishing everything within sight. For once, the Max-wells seem to have been unable to defend their own, and the people of Nithsdale suffered accordingly. In despair at their in-ability to obtain any redress, a deputation of women travelled to Edinburgh, taking with them fifteen bloody sarks taken from the bodies of their murdered husbands. It was in vain, for neither king nor council would listen to them, so the widows decided to demonstrate in the streets of Edinburgh, where the sight of the gory shirts made such an impression on public opinion that James was forced to take action. This he did by ordering the warden (who, of course, was Maxwell) to arrest Johnstone of Dunskellie and, if he would not surrender, attack his castle of Lochwood and 'raze out the memory of him and his name in these bounds".

With a couple of thousand men, Maxwell set off with the intention of carrying out his instructions to the letter, but when he reached the Annan at a point just below its junction with Dryfe Water, he found the Johnstones drawn up in battle array. No sooner had he appeared on the other side of the river than they sent out a screen of horsemen "to ride and make provocation" with the Johnstone warcry of "Ready, aye ready". Maxwell responded by sending his own men for-ward with their usual shout of "Wardlaw, I bid you bide Ward-law". And so began the battle of Dryfe Sands which, after bitter fighting, ended in a victory for the Johnstones, thus upsetting James' plans yet again.

The mixture of horse and foot resulted in a great number of those on foot, and particularly the dismounted fleeing through the streets of Lockerbie, suffering a downward blow on the face, rather than the usual leg wounds, and such in-juries came to be known as "Lockerbie licks". Maxwell him-self was knocked off his horse. Tall as he was, and weighed down with armour he could not get up and was left for dead. What happened next is a matter for conjecture. One version of the story credits Willy Johnstone, the Galliard's nephew, with killing Maxwell and cutting off his arm. Another, and even less attractive, has it that Willy only did the butcher-ing, and that it was the wife of Johnstone of Kirkhill who brained him with the tower keys that hung at her girdle. What-ever the manner of Maxwell's death, it seems fairly certain that his arm was carried away as a trophy and nailed to the wall of the Lochwood.

The battle of Dryfe Sands, with its grisly ending, really settled nothing, and the feud dragged on for another fifteen years. Then the Lord Maxwell of the day proposed a friendly meeting at which he and the chief of the Johnstones could discuss a settlement of the dispute; each to be accompanied by a single attendant. By previous arrangement, Maxwell's companion picked a quarrel with his opposite number and, drawing his dagg, shot him dead. This was the signal for Maxwell to put a couple of bullets into Johnstone's back, which likewise proved fatal. How Maxwell thought he could get away with this sort of conduct is not easy to understand. He was, of course, forced to fly the country; finally making his way to France, where he remained for the next four years, though there is no evidence that he ever repented his evil deed.

> Though I hae slain the Lord Johnstone,
> What care I for their feid?
> My noble mind their wrath disdains.
> He was my father's deid.

But in the end, he was made to care, for on his return to Scotland he was betrayed and executed.

If the quarrels and feuds on the Scottish side of the Border were more spectacular, they were certainly no more frequent than those in England. The life of the younger Scrope, for instance, was made hideous by the apparently endless squabbles in which the Grahams, Carletons and Lowthers indulged; while the gentry of Northumberland were notorious. Among the most hot-blooded of the latter were the Selbys, who nursed a long-standing grudge against the Collingwoods. The feud originated, as in so many cases, from a perfectly legitimate action taken in an official capacity. In this case it was Sir Cuthbert Collingwood, twice sheriff of Northumberland and at one time deputy warden who, having already incurred the lasting enmity of the Scotts of Teviotdale, had accused Sir John Selby of March Treason.

One day in 1586 Collingwood, his wife and family, his son-in-law Robert Clavering (the current sheriff) and ten others, were on their way to Newcastle, at the behest of the President of the Northern Council, to celebrate the anniversary of the queen's accession. At Stanton, near Morpeth, they rode into an ambush laid by Sir John's son William, with a dozen men, most of them drawn from the Berwick garrison. Lady Collingwood threw herself on her knees and begged for mercy, while the sheriff demanded that the queen's peace be observed. It was all in vain. At a place now marked by the 'Clavering Stone' Selby's party discharged their pistols and "shot Sir Cuthbert in the belly and young Clavering, the Sheriff's brother in the breast and out at the back". William Clavering subsequently died of his wounds, but Collingwood recovered. Four of those responsible were arrested, three of whom were convicted of murder; but this proved to be one of the rare occasions when the payment of compensation prevented the inception or continuance of deadly feud, for the Claverings accepted a sum of money and called it a day. The feud between Selbys and Collingwoods, however, rumbled on, while the Selbys were also involved not only in an attempt to murder the captain of the Berwick garrison but in a bloody quarrel with the Greys.

The Greys, in turn, feuded with the Widdringtons, and the Herons with the Carnabys; John Heron being finally compelled to renounce his feud for fear of the law. His connivance with the reivers of Liddesdale in burning William Carnaby's property at Little Whittington and again at Halton, was so obvious that he really had no alternative, other than to be convicted of March Treason for assisting the Scots.

More understandable, and even more widespread, than the domestic feuds were those that extended across the Border. One of the most famous of these was between the Scotts of Buccleuch and the Charltons of Hesleyside, in North Tyne. This culminated in a series of forays which the Bold Buccleuch made between 1594 and 1597, in one of which no less than three hundred took part. Sir John Carey, in his capacity as Marshal of Berwick, was moved to explain to Burghley how the feud had first originated. "Your honour," he wrote, "knows long since, you heard of a great rode that the Scottes, as Will Harkottes and his fellows, made upon Tyndale and Ridsdale, when they took up the whole country and did very nearly beggar them for ever." The Charltons, he went on, had been so incensed by these losses and by "Bucclughe* and the rest

* The grandfather of the current laird.

of the Scottes having made some bragges and crackes" that they had retaliated in kind. Not only had they won back everything that was lost, but they had captured Buccleuch, and kept his sword, which they refused to give up (and incidentally retain to this day at Hesleyside).

It was not only against the Scotts, however, that the Charltons continually waged war: it was also against the Elliots of Liddesdale. The origin of this particular feud had been the striking by Alexander Charlton of his namesake Sandy Elliot "with a dagger in the left side below the arm, whereof Elliot imediately died". Not that it took very much to upset the Elliots for, as Thomas Musgrave once put it, "the Elliots are grown so to seek blood that they will make a quarrel for the death of their grandfather, and then will kill any of the name".

Difficult as it was for authority to bring to an end a feud within its own territory, it must have been infinitely more difficult where both countries were involved. It so happened that in one of the many skirmishes with the Scots in which Sir Cuthbert Collingwood was involved, he, or one of his surname, had killed a Burn. For ten years the Burns waited their opportunity; then took their revenge by raiding the Collingwoods and killing thirty-five of them. In order to settle the feud which was now in full swing, the belligerents arranged for six of one surname to meet six of the other and fight it out. James VI, getting wind of what was going on, forbade the affair and in order to make doubly sure, imprisoned several of the Burns. Collingwood had also been forbidden to take part but, in spite of the injunction, arrived on the field of battle, only of course to find no one there.

There are records in plenty of the number of feuds raging at any one time both within and between England and Scotland; Sir John Forster reporting, for instance, shortly before his retirement, no less than twenty-four Northumberland surnames at feud with ten of their opposite numbers in Scotland.

Sometimes, wholesale revenge could lead to the virtual extermination of a small and defenceless surname or grayne. The Bells, for example, had made themselves so unpopular on the Scottish side of the Border that, like the Armstrongs, many of them were constrained to emigrate to the English side. On one occasion, the Bells of Gilsland went so far as to complain directly to the Privy Council that the Armstrongs (presumably of the Scottish branch) had been harassing them to such an extent that soon there would be none of them left. As they were now tenants of Queen Elizabeth they claimed the protection of the crown before it was too late. In particular, they blamed the Carletons for egging on their persecutors. Burghley, in turn, asked Thomas Carleton for an explanation, and Carleton, who was of course related to the Armstrongs by marriage, was justly indignant. It was ludicrous he protested, to suppose that eighty of the Bells had been beggared, as they claimed: there did not exist as many of that surname in the country.

It was possible, of course, for continual retaliation to take place without a family feud, as such, being created. One night in 1596, a party of Kers stole some sheep belonging to the Parson of Wooler. The parson, in turn, collected a posse and made off with a sheep belonging to Cessford's own shepherd. He may have thought that this token retaliation would be the end of the matter. If so, he was mistaken, for Cessford was so incensed at what he seems to have regarded as a personal insult that he promised to take the parson's life in return. The latter wisely retired to Berwick, where he could enjoy the protection of the garrison. He was only just in time, for "so highlie was Sesfordes honor touched therein" that "with four score horsemen and trumpet sounded" he proceeded to exact revenge by seeking out an inoffensive gentleman called Bolton whom Sir John Ker (Cessford's son) proceeded to murder in cold blood, leaving "the rest of his companie to cut him all in pieces". Two of the Storys, brothers-in-law to the murdered man, retaliated by attacking Cessford's shepherd and carving him up. His master, in return, laid an ambush for the Storys near Weetwood, in the hope of catching them on their way to the Whitsun Fair. On this occasion they managed to escape; but not for long, for in the end the Kers came upon Will Story and obtained their bloody revenge.

It might be thought from the constant stream of complaints made by English officials that it was the Scots alone who kept the Border in a ferment. However, it only requires a cursory examination of the business transacted at days of truce to discover that the damage done by the English reivers was every whit as great, and very often greater. The explanation is, of course, that the English wardens were required to keep in much closer touch with their government than were their Scottish counterparts, and their frequent reports tend to convey a somewhat one-sided impression.

In another such report, written soon after the saga of the Wooler parson, Sir Robert Carey describes a foray which was equally typical of Cessford. As Warden of the East March, Carey had recently had occasion to hang the notorious Geordie Burn, one of the most thoroughgoing scoundrels of his age. Geordie was a protégé of Cessford, who promptly descended on the East March in order to revenge his death. First he drove away a number of cattle, not because he needed them, but simply as bait. When this stratagem failed to bring forth those of whom he was in search, Cessford gave orders for them to be driven back again for, as he said, "it was not cattle but blood he desired".

A classic case of revenge, and of the time and effort lavished on it, concerns a much earlier Ker; this time Sir Robert Ker of Caverton, son of a previous laird of Cessford. Caverton was an important figure in his own country, for he was not only Warden of the Middle March but also Master of the King's Artillery and Principal Cup-bearer. It was in 1511 that he took part in a day of truce at Gamelspath, in the Cheviots, where he was murdered by a party of Englishmen. The perpetrators of the crime, so far as could be ascertained, were John (better known as Bastard) Heron, one of the Lilburns and a gentleman known to history as Starkhead, or Starhead, who may in reality have been the laird of Staward. So far as Lilburn was concerned, retribution was swift and sure, for he was caught and imprisoned in Fast Castle, where he died. The other two, however, were nowhere to be found. In the end, Sir William Heron, Warden of the English Middle March, was forced to surrender himself as surety for his half-brother, who seems to have been no more troubled by the fate of the unfortunate warden than he was at himself being put to the horn. Tradition has it, however, that he subsequently appeared at the battle of Flodden, where he fought so valiantly that Henry VIII remitted his sentence of outlawry.

Meanwhile the Kers were intent on tracking down Starhead. For years the wanted man seems to have moved from place to place all over the north of England, twisting and turning in order to shake off his pursuers. It was all in vain and the Kers, refusing to be cheated of their prey, finally ran him to earth near York, and duly despatched him.

The death which touched off 'deadly feid' usually, but not necessarily, took place during the course of a foray, or of the hot trod that succeeded it. It might also take place, however, as a result of single combat, perhaps arising from the picturesque custom of 'bauchling or reproving'. This was a practical expression of the Borderers' code of honour, which required that a band, whether it was to pay a ransome or carry out some other contract, once entered into, should be implemented, come what may, and that if it were broken the offender should be held up to the execration of his fellow men.

'Bauchling', as it was explained by a contemporary, "is a public reproof, or rather an appeal, by holding a glove (representing the false hand of the person bauchled) on a spear's point, at a day of truce or other assembly of English and Scots, whereby the party bauchled is accused or challenged for breaking his word, faith or bond; and sometimes the spear and glove are by the accuser fixed on the housetop of the person accused." As an alternative, the effigy of the offender might be drawn on a piece of board, which would then be attached (preferably upside down) to the tail of the bauchler's horse.

A typical instance of this practice is to be found at a meeting that was arranged at Spylaw, on the Scottish side of the Border, between commissioners from the two kingdoms, in order to make an exchange of prisoners. A good deal of commotion seems to have been caused on an otherwise decorous occasion by one of the Commissioners, Lance Ker, riding round the gathering, bearing "at his spear's point a glove, and above the same a little paper, being therein written the name of Sir Roger Grey". Apparently the Kers had released Grey on parole, and he had failed to surrender himself when required to do so.

On another occasion, James VI, becoming heartily sick of the antics of certain Grahams, and particularly the lairds of the Peartree and Rosetrees, and the outlaws attached to them, despatched the warden, Lord Herries, "to burn and subdue the fugitives about Gretna". Henry Leigh, Lord Scrope's deputy, was a witness to what happened next, and he reported it all with considerable amusement to his master. Herries 'burnt' among others, one Rob of Langriggs "who was not well content therewith. . . . And thereupon ensued a pretty sport" for he proceeded to "openly baffell and reprove the said Lord Herries of treason by bearing his glove upon a spear point". Rosetrees, who was Rob's uncle, together with the other Grahams and their womenfolk, joined in the fun, and the warden had some difficulty in beating a dignified retreat in the face of a brawling multitude.

When Bernard Gilpin, the Apostle of the North, came to preach at Rothbury, he was horrified to find not only the parties to a feud entering the church with a view to doing battle, but to find a glove actually hanging over the altar. This, the sexton explained, was a perfectly normal method of offering a challenge to a man who was bauchled, or to anyone else who cared to pick it up on his behalf. Gilpin promptly tore it down.

Originally, bauchling had been an officially accepted feature of Border meetings, where anyone who was aggrieved at another breaking his band would ride through the assembly, shouting the name of the offender in order to put him to shame. This was usually so effective that it caused him either to pay up or fight. If he did neither, it was not unknown for him to be executed by his own surname in order to wipe out the disgrace. Hence, perhaps, the clause in the treaty of 1553 which forbade the practice of bauchling except by licence of the wardens. Anyone disobeying this injunction was to be handed over to the opposite warden and to have his bill, if any, automatically filed.

A favourite spot for single combat was at the junction of the Kershope Burn with Liddel Water, known to this day as the Tourneyholme, which was near enough to the Border line to constitute neutral ground if the event were international. Usually, but by no means always, the combatants fought with lances on horseback. One notable exception to this rule was the meeting of Thomas Musgrave, then Captain of Bewcastle, with Lancelot Carleton, who had accused him of offering to betray that place to the Scots. In this case they signed an indenture, which set out the reason for the duel, together with the conditions under which it was to take place. They were to fight on "the 8th day of April next ensuing, A.D. 1602, betwixt nine of the clock and one of the same day, to fight on foot; to be armed with jack, steel cap, plate sleeves, plate breeches,

plate socks, two baslaerd* swords, the blades to be one yard
and half a quarter in length, two Scotch daggers or dirks at their
girdles. ..."

Another exception to the general rule was when Sir Robert
Ker of Cessford challenged Henry Widdrington to meet him
on

> Fryday morning next, being the seventh September, God willing,
> att the Hayr Craggs in the March between England and Scotland
> by eight howers in the morning with a short sword and a
> whyniard†, with a steel bonet and plate sleeves, without any
> more weapons offensive or defensive.

There seems no doubt that the more usual encounters on
horseback often took place in duplicate, so that they could
hardly be described, in the literal sense of the words, as 'single
combat'. The fifth Earl of Bothwell once fought Ker of
Cessford, when their feud was at its height, for two hours
at a stretch; after which they were too tired to continue.
As was so often the case, the heavy armour that they wore
proved impenetrable, but one of the Rutherfords, who was
the Earl's second string, was cut on the cheek by Gibson,
who was Ker's doubles partner.

* Protected as to the handle.
† Or whinger. A kind of dagger.

CHAPTER ELEVEN

Character and Philosophy

For all the beasts of the forest are mine: and so are the cattle upon a thousand hills.

Psalm XLIX

A readiness to embark on single combat, or any other kind of violence, was just one aspect of a philosophy that held life cheaply, but placed great value on courage. Perhaps it was the constant struggle for survival against the elements, and in competition with their fellow men, that made the reivers the stern, uncompromising realists that they were. Above all, they admired courage and strength; as in the case of Red Rowan, "the starkest* man in Teviotdale", on whose shoulders Kinmont Willie was borne out of Carlisle Castle. More than two centuries afterwards, when a young man was courting one of the Hedleys of Redesdale and looking for the consent of the girl's family, her mother was asked to give the casting vote. "Let him come in amongst us," she said, "he's a grand fighter."

Might, indeed, was recognized as right, and the weakest, unless supported by a strong surname, were likely to go to the wall. Typical of the plight in which the individual could in fact find himself is that of "Jamie Telfer of the Fair Dodhead" in the ballad of that name, which begins,

> It fell about the Martinmas tyde,
> When our Border steeds get corn and hay,
> The Captain of Bewcastle hath bound him to ryde
> And he's ower to Tividale to drive a prey.

The expedition made for Liddesdale—

* Strongest.

And when they came to the Fair Dodhead,
Right hastily they clam the peel*;
They loos'd the Kye out, ane and a'
And ranshackled the house right weel.

Now Jamie Telfer's heart was sair,
The tear aye rowing† in his ee;
He pled wi' the captain to hae his gear
Or else revenged he wad be.

The captain turned him round and leugh‡;
Said 'man there's naething in thy house
But ae auld sword without a sheath
That hardly now wad fell a mouse'.

Jamie Telfer's only hope of survival in a bleak world was to get back his cattle—or somebody else's—and there's the rub. There were a limited number of cattle and sheep in the Borders and, subject to pestilence or sudden death, a fixed number of people to live off them. So obvious was this fact that cattle, sheep, horses and goats were regarded almost, if not quite, as a floating population common to all, so that as has already been suggested, 'farming' had become like a game of musical chairs in which everyone reimbursed his losses with someone else's stock and only the weakest or least fortunate was left at the end of the game without any. In this case it was Jamie Telfer who was left without a chair: he must steal or go to the wall. So off he hastened to Gibbie Elliot of Stobs. But Gibbie was not interested.

Gae seek your succour at Branksome Ha'
For succour ye'se get none frae me;
Gae seek your succour where ye paid blackmail,
For man! Ye ne'er paid money to me.

So Jamie plodded on to the Coultart Cleugh where lived his brother-in-law Jock Grieve, who lent him a horse to take him to Catslack Hill and Walter Scott, known as William's Wat, who was a close relative of the Laird of Buccleuch at Branxholm. Gibbie Elliot, of course, was under no obligation to take the hot trod on Jamie's behalf, and thereby risk official retalia-

* Climbed the peel stockade.
† Rolling.
‡ Laughed.

tion. On the other hand Buccleuch was honour-bound to give value for what he had received in protection money.

> He's set his twa sons on coal-black steeds;
> Himsel' upon a freckled grey,
> And they are on wi' Jamie Telfer
> To Branksome Ha' to tak the fraye.
>
> And when they cam to Branksome Ha',
> They shouted a' baith loud and hie,
> Till up and spak him auld Buccleuch,
> Said 'Whae's this brings the fraye to me?'
>
> 'It's I, Jamie Telfer o' the Fair Dodhead,
> And a harried man I think I be.
> There's nought left in the Fair Dodhead
> But a greeting* wife and bairnies three'.

This was enough for "Old Buccleuch" (the story must be set about 1600) and he sent for Willie his son, for Wat of Harden and *his* son and for the lairds (all Scotts of course) of Goldielands, Allanhaugh, Gilmanscleuch and Commonside.

> The Scotts they rade, the Scotts they ran,
> Sae starklie and sae steadilie!
> And aye the ower-word o' the thrang
> Was 'Rise for Branksome readilie'.

Just before the Kershope ford they caught up with the Captain.

> John o' Brigham there was slane,
> And John o' Barlow as I hear say;
> And thirty mae o' the captain's men
> Lay bleeding on the ground that day.
>
> The captain was run thro' the thick of the thigh†.
> And broken was his right leg bane;
> If he had lived a hundred years,
> He had never been loved by woman again.

Encouraged by Watty of the Wudspurs‡ the Scotts rode on to Stanegarth where "they loos'd out a' the Captain's kye". Willie Scott was killed but—

* Weeping.
† A euphemism.
‡ Fiery tempered (cf. Hotspur).

> When they came to the Fair Dodhead
> They were a wellcum sight to see!
> For instead of his ain ten milk kye
> Jamie Telfer has gotten thirty and three.

And that is the end of the story, in the form in which it usually appears. It is only fair to add, however, that there is another edition of the ballad, in which it is the Scotts who shrink from helping Jamie Telfer in his distress, and the Elliots who are the heroes of the tale. The moral, however, remains the same.

Here, then, on both sides of the Border, were men who knew no other way of gaining a living than by breeding livestock and, if they lost them, replenishing their flocks and herds at the expense of others. What differentiated them from other cattle thieves is made plain by old Scott of Satchels, when he wrote (or rather, dictated, for he could not write)—

> The Freebooters venture both life and limb,
> Good wife and bairn and every other thing;
> He must do so, or else must starve and die;
> For all his lively-hood comes from the enemie.

It was, indeed, quite normal, even among the hedesmen of the Border, when the larder was bare, for the lady of the house to despatch her menfolk to replenish it. For instance, the wife of one of the Grahams, according to tradition, used to greet him with the words "Ride, Rowley, ride. Hough's i' the pot". In other words, and in north-country parlance, the larder was reduced to the 'last knockings' and it was time to run a foray if the household were to eat.

In the case of the Charltons of Hesleyside, the hedesman would be confronted, on coming to breakfast, by a large dish which, when he removed the cover, would reveal a single spur.* The same practice was followed by the Scotts at Harden, where dwelt that Walter Scott whose predatory habits have already been mentioned.

Old Wat was a man of many parts. A reiver by inclination and by upbringing, he ran his forays in the grand manner, whether to despoil the English or those on his own side of the Border. Not only was he endowed with the natural bravery of

* Preserved, like Buccleuch's sword, at Hesleyside.

his surname but he added to this a talent for generalship which, if properly directed, might have made a name for him anywhere. Yet he seems to have been just as happy riding to Edinburgh in all the magnificence that the court required, as he was to rob another of his cattle. To Old Wat's other attributes, moreover, was added a business sense which made him one of the most successful reivers, financially speaking, that ever lived.

Only once, it seems, did his eye to the main chance deceive him, and that was when he joined the fifth Earl of Bothwell in his abortive attack on the person of James VI at his Palace of Falkland. When the plan misfired, it was only with the greatest difficulty that Old Wat escaped with his life, and it was not long before the Privy Council gave instructions to "destroy the places, houses, and fortalices of Harden and Dryhope pertaining to the said Walter Scott".

It was, of course, Harden's duty as hedesman to look after the basic requirements of his tenants and retainers; a task which involved the regular filling of the steep-sided ravine in front of Harden tower with other people's nolt. On one occasion, after a raid on Gilsland, the booty amounted to "300 oxen and kye, a horse and a nag", and this was quite a normal dividend to expect from the capital that his 'shareholders' provided in the way of armed service. No booty came amiss to him. As he left his tower one day, the Town Herd was calling the cattle out to pasture and in the course of doing so, shouted, "Send out Wat o' Harden's coo". The fact that his circumstances were so reduced that but a single cow remained stung Old Wat to immediate action. "My sang," he roared, "I'll soon mak ye speak of Wat o' Harden's kye," and, gathering his men together, he set off for England to replenish his stock. Apparently the expedition was successful for they returned with a "bow of kye and a bassened bull*". As he passed a haystack, Old Wat epitomized the reiver's philosophy when he exclaimed, "By my soul, had ye but four feet, ye should not stand lang there!"

Equally characteristic of the Borderer's hard and practical outlook was another remark ascribed to Harden. On returning one day from Edinburgh, he discovered that the Scotts of Gilmanscleuch had come upon his youngest son, when hunting, and killed him. His other five sons were eager for immediate

* A herd of cows and a brindled bull.

"Ferniehirst Castle. . . . Sir John Ker was forced to lay siege to his own home."

"Bauld Willie had succeeded to the Dacre Estates and Naworth Castle."

revenge, but their father, ever with an eye to business, knew better. He locked them up in a dungeon to prevent any precipitate action, and galloped off to Edinburgh. Here he lodged his complaint, and persuaded the king to sequestrate the Gilmansleuch lands and award them to him. "The lands of Gilmansleuch," he is reputed to have said, "are well worth a dead son".

But if reiving was a business, it also enabled the Borderers to satisfy a sporting instinct which is now, perhaps, best expressed in hunting—"the image of war", as Jorrocks put it, "without its guilt, and only five-and-twenty per cent of its danger". Indeed they found nothing dishonourable in gambling their courage and resourcefulness, and ultimately their life, against another's. It followed that proficiency in the arts of robbery and warfare, upon both of which their lives depended, ranked high among the characteristics that the reivers respected. As Sir Robert Bowes put it in his report on the state of the Borders, "they most praise and cherish such as begin soonest in youth to practice themselves in Thefts and Robberies and other semblable enterprises contrary to the king's grace's Laws".

In the same report, Bowes went on to say that the population of Tynedale and Redesdale "had rather live poorly there as thieves than more wealthily in another country". They saw, in fact, nothing strange in making a living by robbing others and Dr Bullen echoed their sentiments pretty accurately when, in a play produced in London in 1654, he made one of his characters say "I was born in Redesdale in Northumberland and come of a wight* riding surname, call'd the Robsons; gude honest men, and true, saving a little shifting for their living. God help them! silly pure† men".

Even James I of England who, when he sat on the Scottish throne, had probably done, or at any rate tried to do, as much as any to discourage the reiving habits of the Borderers, had perhaps a sneaking appreciation of their point of view. Soon after he had travelled south to assume the English throne, his favourite cow broke out and made tracks for Scotland, where she presently arrived safe and sound. One of his courtiers, remarked facetiously how strange it was that, speaking neither English nor Scots, she had managed to find the way. Whereupon

* Strong.
† Frail, poor men.

James drily replied that it "did not excite his wonder so much as how she could get across the Debatable Ground without being stolen".

The fact that the reivers themselves were not inclined to take their crimes too seriously seems to have led a succession of writers to portray them as people not only more carefree, but altogether more chivalrous and noble than they actually were, or had any chance to be. One such even went so far as to write of his ancestors as "an honourable and kind-hearted people, loth to shed blood—in fact a jolly, thoughtless set of marauders". He could hardly have been further from the truth. Honourable they were, in so far as they would keep their word to each other, no matter what might be the consequences, but, as must by now be obvious, the requirement to do so did not extend far outside their own ranks. Kind-hearted, perhaps to their wives and families and, no doubt their horses, but there is no evidence that, apart from hanging together in time of trouble, the reivers were particularly benevolent. In view of the rigours of their life, it would have been strange if they were.

It is true that they were usually disinclined to murder, so long as they could get what they wanted without it, but this was only common sense. On the other hand, deadly feud specifically required them to kill on occasion, and rarely did they appear to shrink from their duty. And to call them 'jolly marauders' was to miss the whole point of the reivers' existence, coloured as it was by the necessity to earn a living in a cruel world. They seem to have possessed, however, the same wry sense of humour, sardonic, often macabre and slanted against themselves, that their descendants have today. Even from the scanty evidence that we possess of these people's lives, we can hardly fail to catch glimpses of their liking for a joke, though it took a good deal, one imagines, to move such 'grim and tragic men' to laughter.

The Armstrongs, no doubt, were greatly tickled at the thought that while Carey was making his famous expedition against them at Tarras Moss, they were engaged in lifting some of the warden's cattle; or to see Jock o' the Side riding side-saddle 'like ony bride' on his return from Newcastle gaol. Indeed many of the reivers' jokes were inspired by their ability to outwit the common enemy, as when Nicholas Rutherford stole five horses from the garrison at Norham under their very noses, or when that notable reiver, "Geordie Black-dowp", earned his nickname. Geordie was returning home to Redesdale one day well satisfied with a foray that he had conducted, when his party was overtaken and roughly handled, and in the scuffle he lost part of his breeches. After his companions had dispersed in order to throw off their pursuers, his horse went lame and he was forced to squat down in the rushes with only his bare backside showing. "An they ken my face," he explained afterwards, "they dinna ken my dowp."

One of the best examples of reiver wit comes from that Archie Armstrong who later became court jester to Charles I. Archie lived at Stubholm, near the River Esk, whence he sallied forth one day to replenish the larder with one of his neighbour's sheep. Having cut its throat and borne it home, he was much put out to see the shepherd approaching the house. Looking round for somewhere to hide the animal, he lit upon the empty cradle, into which he hastily stuffed it. When the shepherd appeared, Archie, according to his own story, managed to dull his suspicions by taking his oath (which he subsequently immortalized in verse), that—

> If e'er I did sae fause a feat
> As thin my niebour's faulds,*
> May I be doom'd the flesh to eat
> This vera cradle haulds.

As for the reivers' bloodthirstiness, it should always be borne in mind that they lived in a violent age, when the troops sent against them were no whit less cruel than they were themselves, and often with less excuse. In a situation where, to misquote Mark Twain, men "earned a precarious living taking one another's cattle", it was a question of 'kill or be killed'. Nor were the authorities behindhand in the matter; the wardens, especially, agreeing with Lord Braxfield, that ferocious Lord of Session, that a reiver would be "nane the waur of a hanging". Indeed, the principle which the authorities very often followed was to execute a man first and ask questions afterwards, later known as Jeddart† Justice.

Even Belted Will‡", by his own admission a south-country-

* Sheep folds.
† Jedburgh.
‡ Lord William Howard.

man unused to Border ways, apparently caught the habit. Tradition has it that, when disturbed in his library at Naworth by one of his retainers reporting that he had captured a reiver "with the red hand", he exclaimed without looking up (like Henry II with Thomas à Becket), "Oh, hang the fellow". And hanged he was. So common was this practice of instant justice, and so deep the prejudice against numbers of the 'riding clans', that Roger North, when accompanying his brother Lord North on circuit, more than half a century after the Union, was still able to comment on it. "The country," he wrote, "is yet very sharp upon thieves," and then went on to describe how a certain Mungo Noble was being tried at Newcastle on no less than four charges "and his lordship was so much a south-country judge as not to think any of them proved. One of the Scottish Commissioners made a long neck towards the judge, and 'my Laird', said he 'send him to huzz and yees neer him mere'."

It has been said that "the Borderers were accustomed to part with life with as little form as civilized men change their garments". Living the precarious life they did, it could hardly have been otherwise and perhaps, as farmers, they should have paid more heed to the farmers' motto : "Live as if you would die to-morrow; farm as if you would live for ever."

Nowhere, except perhaps in 'Armstrong's Goodnight' is the reivers' stoicism in the face of death better illustrated than in 'The Reiver's Goodbye'.

> The widefon wardanis tuik my geir
> And left me nowther horse no meir,
> Nor erdly guid that me belangit.
> Now, walloway! I mon be hangit.

Which may be translated as :

> The gallows-happy wardens took my goods
> And left me neither horse nor mare,
> Nor earthly goods that to me belonged.
> Now, well-a-day! I must be hanged.

Contemporary opinion of the Borderers in general, and the reivers in particular, varied of course according to the point of view. Valentine Browne, who, as Treasurer, spent some years at Berwick, considered them to be wise, able and stout, so long as they were governed by men who were not personally involved, either because of family or estate, but that they were inclined to make long boastful speeches about what they had done for their country. John Udell, after only a couple of months in the Borders, found them "barbarous more of will than of manners, active of person and speech, stout and subtle, inclined to theft and strife, factious and seditious, full of malice and revenge". All found them eloquent in disaster, and Gilnockie, with his pleas to the king with the "graceless face", was no doubt typical of his kind.

Not only did the Borderers' code of honour require them to keep their word to each other but also to give shelter to any fugitive who required it—and particularly if he was fleeing from justice. It was in 1569 that the Earls of Northumberland and Westmorland, together with Leonard Dacre and others, became involved in what came to be known as the Rising of the North. This was the last stand of the Catholic nobility against the new faith (and, incidentally, in support of Mary Queen of Scots) which ended in disaster, so that the Earls had to fly for their lives. With them went the Countess of Northumberland, that figure of romance who was commonly supposed to have been the heart and soul of the rising, so that men talked freely of "the grey mare, the better horse".

First the fugitives sought shelter with Leonard Dacre at Naworth Castle. However, the crafty Leonard, though one of the chief instigators of the rebellion, having so far managed to cover his tracks, now blandly told the Earls that, as traitors, he could not reasonably be expected to harbour them. There was nothing for it but to make for Scotland, and accordingly they rode on into Liddesdale where outlaws were traditionally welcome. They were not disappointed, for Jock Armstrong of the Side, as behoved a nephew of Mangerton, took them in, believing like his chief that it was "a liberty incident to all nations to succour banished men".

The traditional hospitality of the reivers in cases of this sort was marred, however, on this occasion by Cockburn, the "Black Laird" of Ormiston who, having been put to the horn for helping Bothwell, in the latter's words, to send Darnley "fleeing through the air", had now taken to reiving in order to make both ends meet. He, or his servants, not only robbed the Countess and her ladies of jewels, clothing and money but of their horses also, as well as taking those of ten others of the party, all of whom had to be left behind while the Earls made their separate escapes. It was generally considered to be just retribution when the Ormistons subsequently lost what remained of their lands in a dispute with the Kers of Cessford, and the last member of the family finished up as the public hangman.

There are at least two different versions of what happened next. The unknown author of 'A Diurnal of Remarkable Occurrents' who, although writing not long after the event, very often got his facts wrong, has it that Mary's half-brother, the Earl of Moray who, as Regent, was anxious to keep in with Elizabeth, arranged with Martin Elliot for the betrayal and capture of the Earl of Northumberland. Elliot, in turn, sent Eckie Armstrong of the Harelaw to ask the Earl to come and speak with him under tryst. This the Earl did, whereupon he was ambushed and captured by the Regent's men.

If Martin Elliot was indeed involved, his contribution seems to have gone unnoticed, for it is "Hector of Harlaw" alone whose name became a byword for treachery throughout the Borders, so that 'to take Hector's cloak was regarded as the same kind of insult as 'to be a Quisling' would today.

When Robert Constable, himself described as a 'traitorous spy', sat down to eat with a party of Borderers, they told him that "the like shame was never done in Scotland . . . Hector of the Harlaw's head was wished to have been eaten amongst us at supper". The Laird of Clyshe, who eventually handed the Earl over to the Governor of Berwick, received £20 (presumably in sterling) for his trouble. It is not known what reward was paid to the other actors in the drama, which eventually led to Northumberland's execution.

The Earl of Westmorland, having separated from his colleague, was luckier than he, for he found refuge with Ferniehirst. The latter was no friend of the Regent, and it was said that "Moray durst better eat his own lugs than come again to seek Ferniehirst; if he did, he should be fought with ere he came over Soutra Edge".

Another celebrated betrayal, this time by the Armstrongs themselves, was that of Hobbie Noble who, after a freebooting career to which reference is made elsewhere, met his end at "Weary* Carlisle". It seems that the English, anxious to get their hands on Hobbie, who for long enough had been a thorn

* Troublesome.

in their flesh, bribed some of the Armstrongs of Whithaugh, under the leadership of Sim Armstrong of the Mains, to help them to trap him. The bait was a suggestion by the Armstrongs that Hobbie should join them in a foray which they were proposing to run into the Haltwhistle area. Meanwhile the Land Sergeant had told them what was required:

> Gar meet me on the Rodric-haugh*
> And see it be by break o' day
> And we will on to Conscouthart-green†
> For there, I think, we'll get our prey.

And so it turned out.

> Then they hae ta'en brave Hobbie Noble,
> Wi's ain bowstring they band him sae;
> But his gentle heart was ne'er sae sair,
> As when his ain five bound him on the brae.

The abhorrence which the Borderers felt for the crime of betrayal made it such a rarity that only one other instance comes readily to mind, and that is the case of Parcy Reed of Troughend, near Otterburn, who was not only, like Nimrod, a mighty hunter, but hedesman of one of the principal surnames of Redesdale. In this capacity he incurred the emnity of the Halls of nearby Girsonfield who, as members of a larger and more important surname, were upset by his recent appointment as Keeper of Redesdale to the exclusion of one of their own number. Furthermore, he had, in his official capacity, earned the undying hatred of the Croziers of Liddesdale.

The Halls already had the motive to do away with Parcy: the Croziers would supply the means, and all that was so far lacking was the opportunity. This was provided by a foray that the Croziers were rumoured to be plotting, which would fall in neatly with Parcy's own invitation to the Halls to come hunting with him. When the Keeper called in at Girsonfield for a bite of supper and a word about the next day's sport, he does not seem to have noticed that the loaf of bread was upside down—a bad omen if ever there was one. Meanwhile the Halls took care to damp the primings of his firearm and to jam his sword in the sheath‡ before bidding him goodnight. In the words of the ballad:

---

* Rotheryhaugh, on the Irthing.
† Scotscoultard, nearby.
‡ Perhaps, as in the case of Ringan Armstrong, with yolk of egg.

> They've stown the bridle off his steed
> And they've put water in his lang gun.
> They've fixed his sword within the sheath,
> That out again it winna come.

Next day Parcy rode off in company with the "three fause Ha's of Girsonfield". When they reached Batinghope, a lonely glen under the shadow of Carter Fell, the party stopped to rest and bait their horses. Presently the Halls announced that they could see a party of Croziers approaching over the fells. Parcy Reed, as keeper of the valley, felt it his duty to face up to them, but the Halls would have none of it.

> We mayna stand, we canna stand,
> We dairna stand alang wi' thee;
> The Crosiers haud thee at a feud
> And they wad kill baith thee and we.

Unable to separate his sword from the scabbard in which it was 'fangit', or to fire his gun (some say it blew up), Parcy Reed was no match for the Croziers.

> They fell upon him all at once,
> They mangled him most cruellie,
>
> The slightest wound might cause his deid
> And they hae given him thirty three.
> They hackit off his hands and feet
> And left him lying on the lea.
>
> 'Now Parcy Reed, we've paid our debt;
> Ye canna well dispute the tale'.
> The Crosiers said, and off they rade
> They rade the airt* of Liddesdale.

And so the remains of Parcy were taken home in a sheet; but the treachery of the Halls was not so easily disposed of. For years after the event, any of the Halls who asked for hospitality within their own county might expect to find the cheese (not the loaf this time) placed before them upside down —an accepted sign of disrespect. It was well into the nineteenth century, indeed, when a traveller asked the landlord of the inn at Horsley, in Redesdale, what was his name. "Wey, noo," answered the innkeeper, "Aa winna disguise me neame: me

* Direction.

neame's Ha' . . . Tommy Ha'," whereupon he wept copiously into the beer, denying all the while that there was any relationship with the traitors of Girsonfield.

The corollary to the Borderers' horror of betrayal was, of course, their loyalty to each other, which they were quite prepared to extend also to those whom they happened to befriend. Robert Constable, the spy, for instance, marvelled that although "they are my guides, and outlaws who might gain their pardon by surrendering me, yet I am sure of their fidelity, and we have often proved it". According to Bishop Ridley, "the more steadfastly a man stuck by his neighbour in the fight . . . the more fervour and friendship shall all his posterity have for the slain man's sake of all them that be true, as long as the memory of his fact and his posterity doth endure".

Giving one's word to a friend, or even an enemy, was one thing, however; to give it to officialdom was quite another. Yet officialdom seems never to have quite appreciated the difference. Thomas, Lord Scrope, insisted that all Borderers were accustomed to false swearing, while Bowes and Ellerker, in their report on the state of the Borders, accused those on the Scottish side of telling more lies than truth.

But, if chivalry, in its widest sense, spells fair-dealing and loyalty, the fact remains that it is primarily concerned with man's respect for womankind, and no attempt to describe the reivers' philosophy would be complete without some mention of the role of women in the life of the Borders. There is no doubt that if the men's existence was stern and dangerous, it was their women who had the hardest cross to bear for, like that of Lorraine, it was a double one. In the first place, when her menfolk set out on a foray or hot trod, a woman would not only be concerned lest they failed to replenish the larder, but might well be racked with fear for their safety, despite the assurance that if anything went wrong the surname would see that she did not starve. Such suspense must have been very hard to bear, and it is not surprising that it bred a kind of callousness, or at any rate resignation. In the second place there was the ever-present fear that, whether the husband was himself a reiver or the most innocent of men, a party of thieves might descend on the place in his absence, bent on robbery and violence.

Pius II, before his accession to the papal throne, had occasion to spend a night on the English side of the Border. A rumour arose that a raid was on the way, but he was assured that the Scots did not harm non-combatants or women. He noticed, nevertheless, that the women made for the woods as fast as they possibly could. Odd things could happen if they stayed, as on the occasion when a number of reivers broke into the house of Robert Unthank at Melkridge, in Tynedale, and shut up his daughter Alicia in an ark.*

A Borderer returning home from his lawful occasions could never be certain that he would not find his cattle and insight lifted and his house a blackened shell. On the other hand, despite impressive phrases to the effect that "no man's life and no woman's honour was safe" there is little evidence that rape was one of the reivers' normal pastimes: perhaps they were in too much of a hurry.

Furthermore, it seems to have been a rare event for women to be carried off as prisoners, though it was difficult for them to remain uninvolved when an extensive raid was in progress. In 1611, for example, a number of Armstrongs and Elliots ran a foray against the Robsons of Leaplish in North Tyne, a place which is now represented only by the ruins of a shepherd's cottage. In the course of the fray, "Elizabeth Yearowe was shott with twoe bullettes through both her thighes, the right thighe broken asunder with the shott, and slaine. Mane Robson, wife to James Robson, called Blackehead is shott with fyve haileshott in her breastes," and "Elizabeth Robson . . . being great with childe, is hurte verie sore in the head with the stroke of a peece."

Most of the female casualties, however, seem to have come about more or less accidentally; particularly where fire was employed. In 1532, for instance, the Earl of Northumberland reported that "the Scots burned a town of mine called Alnham with all the corn, hay and household stuff in the said town," and, rather as an afterthought, "also a woman". An exception was when Mark Ker had promised the Earl "to burn a town of mine within three mile of my poor house of Warkworth where I lie, and give me light to put on my clothes at midnight". Accordingly, he attacked "a littel village of myne called Whitell . . . upon Shipbotel† moor". Finding, however, when

---

* Chest or corn-bin.
† Shilbottle.

the time came, that they had "no flint and fizzle" with them, the Kers murdered a pregnant woman and made off again.

The attitude of those in authority to the slaughtering of women seems to have been as equivocal as it was towards other acts of violence, which they condemned in others while acting in much the same way themselves. When Gilnockie and his followers were executed, for instance, one of them was burnt alive instead of being hanged, as having been responsible for the death by fire of women and children. Yet when Lord Grey of Wilton was Warden of the East March of England, he thought nothing of burning the tower of Catslack, in Yarrow, with the aged Lady Buccleuch inside, and of burning another woman in his assault on Newark Tower. In acting like this the warden was only following the example of, for instance, the Earl of Hertford who, as Lieutenant General in the North, spared neither man, woman nor child, when he invaded Scotland. The reivers were, in this respect, less callous, if anything, than their betters.

So much for women in the role of victims; but it was not always thus. As in the case of the Grahams of Netherby, the Charltons of Hesleyside, the Scotts of Harden, and many other families, it was the lady of the house who, for economic reasons, was often the instigator of "theft and stouthreif".* It was not unknown, moreover, for a female to do battle in person. Janet, Lady Buccleuch, who was popularly supposed to have encouraged the queen to accede to Darnley's murder, rode at the head of her son's grayne when they raided the Kirk of St Mary of the Lowes, in their feud with the Cranstouns. And was it not the wife of Johnstone of Kirkhill who was reputed to have "dinged in the harns†" of Lord Maxwell with her tower keys after the battle of Dryfe Sands?

It was in defence, however, rather than in attack, that the role of a Borderer's wife was most evident, and what could be done in this way has never been better illustrated than in that curiously named ballad, 'The Fray of Suport' which, in fact, describes a raid on Solport, a few miles east of Longtown. Scott calls the ballad "an ancient border gathering song", and goes on to say, "of all the Border ditties which have fallen into the Editor's hands, this is by far the most uncouth and savage. It

* Robbery with violence.
† Battered out the brains.

is usually chanted in a sort of wild recitative, except the burden, which swells into a long and varied howl, not unlike to a view hollo' ". This 'burden', represented by "a', a', a', a', a', a' ", seems to have been the war-whoop, or gathering cry, designed to summon those who were required to follow the hot trod.

The ballad is put into the mouth of a woman who has just lost her all to some Scottish reivers, and is not prepared to sit down and lament her loss, but prefers to take violent action.

Weel may ye ken,
Last night I was right scarce o' men:
But Toppet Hob o' the Mains had guestened in my
                                    house by chance;
I set him to wear [guard] the fore-door wi' the spear,
                    while I kept the back door wi' the lance;
But they hae run him thro' the thick o' the thie
                            and broke his knee pan,
And the mergh [marrow] o' his shin-bane has run down on his
                        spur-leather whang [thong]
He's lame while he lives and where'er he may gang.
Fy, lads! shout a', a', a', a', a', a',
My gear's a' gane.

The widow, if widow she was, is left not only with her gear all gone but with a 'toom byre' (in other words an empty cow-house); yet the neighbours still slumber on. The reivers have got away, but they must travel slowly if they are to keep the stolen cattle with them, so she wakes those living nearest her and alerts the watchers at each of the fords between her and the Border. Then she summons Cuddy of the Heugh Head with his ammunition bag of brock [badger] skin, and Dan of the Howlet Hirst who is "gude wi' a bow and better wi' a spear".

Rise, ye carle [boorish] coopers, frae making
                        o' kirns [churns] and tubs,
In the Nicol forest woods.
        If you had only fear of God,
        Last night, ye hadna slept sae sound.
        Fy, lads! shout a', a', a', a', a', a',
        My gear's a' gane.

Finally, to the lady's relief, the Captain of Bewcastle comes to the rescue.

Captain Musgrave and a' his band
Are coming down by the Siller strand,
And the muckle town bell of Carlisle is rung;
My gear was a' weel won
And before it's carried o'er the Border,
Mony a man's gae down.
Fy, lads! shout a', a', a', a', a', a',
My gear's a' gane.

And off they all go in pursuit of the reivers.

CHAPTER TWELVE

Effect of Religion, if Any

Penance, father, will I none;
Prayer know I hardly one.
Sir Walter Scott, *The Lay of the last Minstrel*

It may be thought that where the Borderers' womenfolk had failed to exert a moderating influence, religion might have succeeded; but for a number of reasons this was not the case. To begin with, the unreformed Church was so rife with abuses that even if there had been enough priests in the Borders, and even if they had stayed in their parishes, their personal example was not likely to impress the Borderers with the value they might derive from religion. All that many of them could offer, in fact, was a certain amount of lipservice to the teaching of the Church, and a good deal of superstition.

The Reformation, when it came, was slow to affect the situation, except for the worse. Nor did this state of affairs, generally speaking, alter very much throughout the sixteenth century. For long enough, indeed, Catholicism lingered on in the Borders; partly because of the influence of a reactionary nobility, and partly because of the sheer lack of clergy who could, or would, take the place of those who would not conform.

In Northumberland the Reformation actually went into reverse. As early as 1569 'popish priests' galore were going to earth in the houses of the gentry, and Sir Ralph Sadler was moved to remark that there were not more than ten gentlemen in the county who respected the Queen's requirements regarding religion. Soon, Father Sheppard was saying mass openly in the Percy stronghold of Warkworth, and the Jesuits had

achieved a counter-reformation in miniature; the total of
Protestant gentlemen in the East Marches having apparently
fallen to three. One of these, presumably, was Sir John Forster,
who no doubt cared little one way or another, but whose
apparent orthodoxy so annoyed the Collingwoods. It was
reported that many of the ladies of the county were "notorious
recusants" but, like their husbands, they probably conformed
outwardly to the new faith by attending church once a quarter.
Sir Robert Carey was later to report to Burghley, "I am to
advise your Lordship that in long and often laying of bait I
have at last caught a fish (but not the same I fain would have
had). This is one Mr Thomas Ogleby, a seminary priest lately
come out of Flanders".

In Bernard Gilpin's day, as we have seen, the Borderers had
no great respect either for churches or for those who ministered
to them, and were not averse to pursuing their brawls on holy
ground. Lady Buccleuch, when she found that the Cranstouns
had gone to ground in the kirk, promptly burnt it down. When
five hundred from Liddesdale laid waste to Ryle, Prendwick
and Reaveley under Sir John Forster's nose, they improved the
occasion by tearing down, and presumably carrying away, the
lead from the roof of Ingram church. No wonder that when
St Cuthbert's church at Bellingham was renovated in 1609, only
a few years after some Scottish reivers had "spoiled the townsmen and brake the cross", the roof was vaulted in stone in
order to leave nothing inflammable.

To be fair, however, the despoiling of churches was in no
way a prerogative of the reivers, for English generals seem to
have taken a special delight in destroying the sacred edifices of
Scotland. Eure and Layton, for instance, laid waste to Melrose
Abbey and, as if this were not sacrilege enough, the Earl of
Hertford repeated the offence.

The reivers' attitude towards the clergy was much the same
as towards their churches : they seem to have had scant respect
for them. In 1528, for example, William Charlton of Shitlington,
in North Tyne, together with Archie Dodd and a couple of
Scotsmen in the shape of Harry Noble and Robert Armstrong,
who had probably been outlawed from Liddesdale, conceived
the idea of riding a foray into the domains of the Bishop of
Durham. Up to a point the expedition seems to have gone
smoothly. They reached the neighbourhood of Wolsingham, in

Weardale, where they not only picked up an appreciable amount of loot but also kidnapped the parson of Muggleswick. On the return journey they broke into three houses and took all the insight; but then their luck changed, for on their arrival at Haydon Bridge they found the South Tyne in flood and the bridge itself securely chained. Worse was to follow, for Thomas Errington, the Earl of Northumberland's bailiff, who had been lying in wait, complete with slue-dog, now raised the hue and cry. In the pursuit that followed, the bailiff, to the subsequent astonishment of the warden and his officers, was ably assisted by another William Charlton, "which forwardness in oppressing mallifactors hath not been sene aforetyme in Tyndaill men". The reivers were finally overhauled, the laird of Shitlington killed by the bailiff in person, and Armstrong and Dodd caught and executed.

That this was not an isolated instance is confirmed by the frequent references in Border history to such events as the kidnapping of the Earl of Hertford's chaplain from Belford and "Jock Pringle that took Parson Ogle".

If there was one family that delighted more than another in harrying the Church, it was those same Lisles who later helped in the rescue of Jock o' the Side. Originally the leading family of Redesdale, they had emigrated to Felton, a few miles south of Alnwick, where successive knights and their progeny kept up a running battle with the canons of Brinkburn Priory. It was in 1514 that the sorely harassed prior complained that a number of the brethren had been put in the stocks by Sir Humphrey Lisle's men, whose master had expelled the Vicar of Felton (who was also a canon of Brinkburn) from his living, and substituted a secular priest. The unfortunate vicar did not dare, for fear of the Lisles, to do anything about the matter, other than weep on the prior's shoulder, and his timidity may well have inspired the rhyme that has been sung in nurseries all over England.

> The little priest of Felton,
> The little priest of Felton,
> He killed a mouse within his house,
> And nobody there to help him.

Worse, however, was in store, for some nine years later, Sir Humphrey's grandson (another Humphrey), together with a certain Jowsey, were indicted for the "cruel murder of Sir Richard Lighton, canon of Brinkburn".

Not unnaturally, the Church was concerned by a situation in which priests were treated with such blatant disrespect. Nor was it prepared to watch indefinitely the continued robberies, burnings and killings by the lay population, which seemed only to increase as time went on. In 1467 a party of Scots had annoyed the Archbishop of York by burning Acomb, a 'town' near Corbridge that was the property of the see of York. It was bad enough when they burnt other people's property, but this was really too much, and the archbishop promptly excommunicated the offenders.

It was Richard Fox, the Prince Bishop of Durham, who was the next to be stung into action and, following repeated forays into his bishopric by the reivers of Tynedale and Redesdale, he issued a "Monition against the notorious robbers of Tynedale". This included what was known as a 'greater', as opposed to a 'lesser', excommunication, and therefore involved the civil power as well as the Church. It accused the majority of the inhabitants of both districts of being either thieves themselves, or the recetters of what was stolen, and it blamed the hedesmen in particular for condoning their sins, not only out of loyalty to the surname but because they shared in the plunder. A great number of those against whom the Monition was directed were excommunicated by name. Soon afterwards, however, some were re-admitted to the Church on condition that they abstained (pious hope!) from all theft in the future, never again wore jack or knapscall* or rode a horse worth more than 6s 8d except against the Scots or the King's enemies. "Nor shall they enter a church, or place consecrated to God, with any weapons exceeding the length of one cubit."†

The laity, however, were not the only people to receive the rough side of Bishop Fox's tongue: the clergy also shared in the broadside for, as he wrote, they were most evil.

They keep their concubines; they are irregular, suspended, excommunicated and interdicted clergy, ignorant almost entirely of letters, so that for ten years they cannot read the words of the mass, as we have proved by examinations of them. And some are not ordained at all, but merely counterfeits of priests, and

* Steel cap.
† About 20 inches.

they dare to celebrate the Holy Sacrifice in profane and ruined places, with vestments torn, ragged and most filthy, unworthy of divine worship, as though a contempt of God. And the said chaplains administer the sacraments to these said thieves, without compelling them to restitution, and bury them in a consecrated ground, against the laws of the church.

By 1524, or thereabouts, the behaviour of such priests as there were in Tynedale had become so scandalous as to move Cardinal Wolsey to put "that evil country" under interdict. Hector Charlton, for one, refused to take the consequent suspension of church services lying down and, either from genuine religious feeling or from sheer devilment, persuaded an itinerant Scottish priest, to say mass while he himself "reserved the parson's duties and served them all of wine".

It was at much the same time that Gavin Dunbar, the Archbishop of Glasgow, also came to the end of his patience. Now an excommunication, whether of greater or lesser degree, has one redeeming feature from the point of view of the transgressor: it is a punishment, in that it removes him from the fellowship of the Church and, to some degree, from that of other men; but at least it can be revoked. Dunbar must have been even more sorely tried than the English clerics for, instead of being satisfied with mere excommunication, he perpetrated a really shattering Curse, or Commination which, once having taken effect, could not, of course, be undone.

This was to be read in every pulpit, and it began, "Gude folks, hear at my Lord Archbishop of Glasgow's letters under his round seal". It then went on in the broadest Scots to wish on its victims every sort of evil thing that had come to pass since the world began, and proceeded to curse by name every little bit of them, adding, in case anything had been left out, "every part of their body from the top of their head to the sole of their feet, before and behind, within and without". They were cursed when sitting, standing, eating, drinking, at home and abroad, together with wives, families, crops, livestock; even to the implements they used on their farms. Thunder and lightning were called down upon them, together with all the plagues of Egypt. The good Archbishop expanded this slightly by hoping that "the Water of Tweed and other waters where they ride may drown them", and that they should be caught by the hair like Absalom. No-one was to speak, eat or drink with them under pain of deadly sin.

And finally I CONDEMN them perpetually to the deep pit of hell, to remain with Lucifer and all his fellows and their bodies to the gallows of the Burrow Muir, first to be hanged, then riven and torn with dogs, swine and other wild beasts, abominable to all the world. . . .

This splendid commination, extending as it did to some fifteen hundred words, neglected only to curse the Scottish reivers, at whom it was directed, "in coughing, in sneezing, in winking"; otherwise it was very reminiscent of the curse laid on the Jackdaw of Rheims (which it may well have begotten) for

> Never was heard such a terrible curse!
> But what gave rise to no little surprise,
> Nobody seemed one penny the worse.

In fact the reivers just laughed at it, as their fellows on the other side of the Border had laughed at excommunication and interdict.

Even if the Borderers had wanted to enjoy the rites of Mother Church it would not have been easy, for not only did the Reformation serve to decrease the number of clergy available, but it became increasingly difficult to find men prepared to brave the risks they were likely to incur in the Borders. Ministers and preachers alike found it "comfortless to come and remain where such heathenish people are", and the Reverend Mr Crackenthorp of Oxford, for example, refused point-blank the living of Simonburn in North Tyne; "deeming his body unable to live in so troublesome a place, and his nature not well brooking the perverse nature of so crooked a people". Perhaps it was not surprising that the clergy that survived were, as often as not, a bastard breed of doubtful orthodoxy and little education, who paid lipservice to the Reformation, when it came, only to retain their benefices.

From this unfortunate state of affairs, there sprang two customs peculiar to the Border and other wild regions. The first involved the itinerant, or 'book-a-bosom' parson, so called because he travelled the Borders from his base at Melrose or elsewhere, with the Book of the Mass stowed in his clothing, holding services, marrying and christening as he went (and it was one of these, of course, who helped Hector Charlton out). Burials seem to have required scant ceremony—probably because in such a warlike countryside, they were all too common. It was the custom, among the Armstrongs at least, to bury the dead within their towers, as at Hollows, where the Dead Stone is still to be seen. However, it was not always the reiver's lot to be buried at home for, often enough, he finished upon the gallows. Whellan, for instance, in his *History of Cumberland*, mentions a visitor to Bewcastle, who asked his female guide why nearly all the tombstones bore women's names and so few men's. "Oh, sir," was the reply, "the men are a' buried at that weary Caerl*."

The second custom was a product of the first, for if a priest was perhaps available only once a year, a problem inevitably arose for those who wished to get married out of season, as it were. The answer was 'handfasting'. This was a custom whereby a couple would live together till the book-a-bosom man could bless their union. The arrangement was for a trial period of one year (unless the parson appeared earlier), after which it became permanent. If, before then, one or other wanted to bring the arrangement to an end, he or she must accept the responsibility for any children of the union, in which case they were still regarded as legitimate. There is still in existence an old genealogy of the Elliots of Larriston, which refers to "Simon of Benks who handfasted or took for a trial a bastard daughter of the said Gibbie with the Golden Garters on condition he should pay her a considerable tocher in case he was not pleased with her". Normally, handfasting required no dowry, and this idea of making second-hand goods more marriageable may well have been restricted to the gentry, who appear to have handfasted in the same way as anyone else. John, Lord Maxwell, for instance, was contracted thus to a sister of the Earl of Angus.

Nobody in the Borders seems to have worried very much about children being born out of wedlock, and there are countless examples of natural children figuring openly in men's wills. When they were not thus provided for, it seems highly probable that, having no land to farm, they swelled the ranks of the broken men whose only source of livelihood was reiving.

* Carlisle.

Altogether the reivers' faith, like that of many of their more respectable brethren was, to say the least of it, primitive. It was alleged, for instance, that the only grace they knew was a strictly businesslike one, namely:

> He that ordained us to be born,
> Send us more meat for the morn:
> Part of't right and part of't wrang,
> God never let us fast ow'r lang.
> God be thanked, and our Lady,
> All is done that we had ready.

Certainly, Bishop Leslie was of the opinion that the reivers never told their beads with so much devotion as when setting out on a foray. They seem to have regarded it as a kind of investment on which they expected a good dividend.

If the Borderers' attitude towards religion left a good deal to be desired, that of the clergy themselves cannot have invited much respect for the cloth. Indeed the nearest that many of the reivers probably came to the real thing was when they 'sang neck-verse at Harribee'; in other words, when they stood under the 'widdie' on Carlisle's Harraby Hill, with the halter already round their necks, listening to a priest reciting the Miserere, or fifty-first psalm.

It would be neither fair nor reasonable, indeed, to criticize the reivers in this respect without looking at the example that was set them. That the standard set was not a very high one was largely the result of a struggle for survival which was hardly conducive to religious fervour. So dangerously had the clergy been forced to live that it was quite normal for them not only to go armed but to be provided with a tower into which they might retreat and defend themselves if required. 'Vicars' Peels' are to be found to this day at Alnham, Elsdon and elsewhere, with a particularly fine one at Corbridge. They found themselves, in fact, in a cleft stick, for they were expected by the civil power to play their part with their parishioners against the reivers of both nationalities, while incurring, as we have seen, the displeasure of their superiors if they did so. A particular bone of contention must have been the inclusion of clergy in the watches which, by Border Law, must be kept on the fords and passes. At Simonburn, for example, "Sir John Hall, priest", was included as a matter of course.

In the circumstances, it is not entirely surprising to find some of the clergy using their training in warfare to make a little on the side. In Bewcastle, for instance, where virtually every able-bodied male was engaged in reiving at some time or other (and in that barren countryside the temptation must have been very strong), it was difficult for the parson to escape the general contamination, despite the presence of the captain and his garrison nearby. Evidence that, on occasion, he succumbed to temptation is to be found in the list of some five hundred names of Englishmen against whom the Scots were complaining in 1552. This begins with a long list of Grahams, including George of the Gingles, alias Henharrow, together with Will Patrick, priest of Bewcastle and also, regrettably, his curate, John Nelson.

The Rev. Thomas Moir, the minister of Morebattle, was another cleric with somewhat unclerical leanings. On one occasion, for example, it was alleged that he had invaded the lands of Toft and, armed with a pitchfork, attacked Andrew, son of Sir John Ker, and also George Pott. He apparently wounded Pott in the face and then upset a cartload of corn into the river. On being confronted by Ker, the parson promptly challenged him to single combat, but met with a refusal; "not," said Andrew, virtuously, "through fear, but through reverence of the Laws". Deprived of his human prey, Moir collected some twenty sympathizers and broke into the barn at Cowbog, stole some corn and, being confronted with Wattie Pott, nearly killed him (or so the latter swore).

Such goings on, however, must be viewed against the background of events in the remainder of the two countries, and especially Scotland. Here, Cardinal Beaton was notorious for his excesses, while the Bishop of the Isles created such a scandal by his armed attacks on other people's estates that he was actually put to the horn. The Bishop of Dunkeld, moreover, confessed that he had never read his Bible. There is no evidence, indeed, that the state of the Scottish Church had improved very much since 1455 when the terms of a certain chaplain's appointment required him to bind himself and six sureties that he would not pawn the sacred plate, books and vestments; to "use no unreasonable excess", and "to have no continual concubine". Presumably an occasional lapse in this respect was acceptable.

Sad to say, the efforts of Archbishops and Bishops to improve the state of the Border clergy seem to have borne remarkably little fruit. By the end of the sixteenth century absenteeism was only too common. The incumbent of Newburn, but a few miles from the city of Newcastle, visited his parish only occasionally, preferring to hire a curate to take his services, and of course to collect the tithes. At Mitford, not far away, the vicar failed to appear altogether; leaving his parish to "a Scotch prieste". Small wonder that respect for the church was at a low ebb or that the Vicar of Tughall, for instance, went in fear of his own parishioners.

CHAPTER THIRTEEN

To-Names

Bright with names that men remember, loud with names that men forget.

A. C. Swinburne, 'Eton, an Ode'

In a countryside where surnames (in the Border sense) were large, and therefore few in number, and christian names restricted, the chances of distinguishing between dozens of Jock Armstrongs, Davie Croziers and Will Charltons were obviously minimal. One solution was to call a man by his christian name, together with that of his farm, so that various Armstrongs appear as Hector of the Harelaw, Jock o' the Side and Sim of the Cathills, and other notable reivers as Tom of the Cavis, Larry Whisgills, Jocke of the Grand Snowke and so forth.

But this method did not cater for the lairds' sons or for landless men, and so there came into use, as in Cumberland, where it had been a Norse custom, that of alluding to people by the christian name of their father as well as their own. The sons of the Armstrongs in question, therefore, might well be known as Eckies Thom, Jocks Sandy and Sims Davie. The use of the mother's name was a fairly common alternative, if only because of the number of births that were either posthumous or the result of a handfasting which had not been followed by marriage. The result was such names as Jenets Watte (Walter), Bessies wifs Riche, Kates Adam, Agnes Cristie, Peggies Wattie, Nanse Archie, Bessies Andrew, and so forth, and just as the laird's son might be known as the Lairds Jock, so might his widow's child be described as the Ladys Hob (Robert). It was still possible, however, for there to be (say) two or three Elliots known as Jocks Cristie living at the same time. In that case it was necessary to introduce another generation and produce results like Jocks Cristies Jock, Sandies Rinyons Archie, Gibbs Geordies Francie, Martins Gibbs Andrew or even Dicks Davies Davie.

An alternative was to use what in the south of England would have been called 'an eke-name'* but, in the Borders, was alluded to both in conversation and in official documents as a 'to-name'. The most obvious kind would be one which described the subject's physical appearance, such as Greathead for Will Crozier, Parke Syppling (Sapling from the Wood) for Henry Robson, Fat Sow for Andrew Hall and Blasteis Jok for someone who was a dwarf; while that notorious freebooter Jerry Charlton was known, from his tuft of hair, as Topping, and John Armstrong, from his squint, as Gleed John. A variation on this theme likened men to various animals, birds and insects such as that "sandy-whiskered gentleman" Elder Will the Tod, and others nicknamed Pyot (Magpie) and Cleg (horsefly).

Anyone who has studied the warfare of the Border must have been struck with the delight that its inhabitants seem to have taken in carving their enemies up. Robert Loraine of Kirkharle in Northumberland, for instance, whose duty it was to keep a supply of horses for the Border service, was so disliked by the Scots that they vowed to "cut him as small as flesh for the pot". They ambushed him one Sunday morning on his way back from church and fulfilled their promise to the letter, a crime commemorated by the inscription on a stone that still stands in the park at Kirkharle.

When the "three fause Ha's of Girsonfield" betrayed Parcy Reed to the Scottish Croziers, it will be remembered that "they mangled him most cruellie", his remains being carried home in a sheet. The same method of transport was used for one of the giant Reay brothers of Gallowshill (also in Northumberland) who was so sure of his own strength that he attacked a party of Scottish reivers single-handed and was "cut into collops"† for his trouble. Over and over again the same, or similar, expressions appear in Border history. At one moment it is a party of Scots who have visited John Selby of Tynedale and, without any known quarrel "cut him all to pieces". At another, "young Mr Haggerston, Thomas Burrell and manie others were most cruelly mangled". During the interminable

---

* Now corrupted to a nickname.
† Slices.

feud between Maxwells and Johnstones, the Lord Maxwell of the day, in his capacity as warden, delivered one of the Johnstones to Lord Dacre for execution. Many years later a gang of Johnstones and Irwins retaliated by seizing a Maxwell, brother of Lord Herries, who had not even been born when the feud originated, and "most cruellie murdered and mangled him, hewinge him to pieces with their swordes".

Nor was this craze for mutilation confined to the ordinary run-of-the-mill reiver. In Buccleuch's great raid into Tynedale, for instance, the Bishop of Durham complained that he spared "neither age nor sex; he cruelly murthered and slue XXXV of her Majesties subjects . . . of which number some he cutt in pieces with his owne handes".

Though the reivers, like their betters, saw nothing particularly reprehensible in cutting their enemies into collops, there is little evidence that they were specially addicted to torture, though occasional instances are recorded. One such victim was Sowerby of Caldbeck, whose house had been broken into, and who complained, as well he might, that his assailants "set him on his bare buttocks upon an hot iron and then they burned him with an hot girdle about his belly, and sundry other parts of his body, to make him give up his money, which they took, under £4".

When Sir John Forster's enemies were trying to oust him from the wardenship of the Middle March, witnesses testified to the great number of "true and able subjects" murdered by the Scots in defence of their own goods. Many of them, they said, had also been taken prisoner, "which prisoners hath been also extremely tortured and pinched, by thrusting hot irons into their legs and other parts of their body, and fettering them naked in the wilderness and deserts by chains of iron to trees, whereby they might be eaten up with midges and flies in summer and in winter perished with extreme cold". A variation of this treatment was to perch the prisoners on the spikes of a harrow tied to the branches of a tree overhanging a river. On the whole, however, prisoners in a position to pay any kind of ransom were probably too valuable to be exposed to undue risk unless, perhaps, in order to find out how much they owned.

It was in the heat of battle, no doubt, that the worst atrocities occurred. When the Duke of Somerset invaded Scotland in 1548, with a mixed force that included mercenaries from a number of countries, he succeeded in capturing Ferniehirst Castle, and the owner, Sir John Ker, was forced to lay siege to his own home. It was to the French troops supporting him, however, that the garrison of English and Spaniards chose to surrender for, in view of their own excesses, they could expect little mercy from the Scots. One of the Borderers, whose wife had been raped, nevertheless approached near enough to the garrison commander to strike his head so that it flew several yards from his body: then bathed his hands in the blood.

All hell seems then to have been let loose, "the Scots contending who amongst them had the art to cut off the leg or the arm of an Englishman with greatest facility" and, where they could not find a prisoner to carve up, buying one from the French. The eye-witness to all this, himself a Frenchman, goes on to describe how the victors tied a wretched captive head-to-heels and then "run upon him with their lances, arm'd as they were, and on horseback, bris'd* him, cut his body to pieces, and carried the divided parcels on the sharp end of their spears. I cannot greatly praise the Scots for this practice." Apparently oblivious of his own contribution to the bloodbath, the gallant Frenchman then went on to emphasize, what was obviously the truth, that it was the excesses of Somerset's own army that were at the root of the trouble. Indeed it would have been remarkable if those on either side of the Border had proved more humane than their masters.

It was soon after Flodden that a major quarrel developed between the Homes and the Duke of Albany, who had been responsible for the execution of Lord Home and at least one of his brothers, and for appointing an outsider to the wardenship that had been hereditary to the family for so long. This was Sir Anthony Darcy, a man of such charm and accomplishments that, in his native France he had been known as the Sieur de la Beauté, and who incidentally turned out to be an extremely efficient warden. Revenge was almost inevitable, but the Homes bided their time until one September day in 1517 when the Frenchman was riding from Dunbar to hold a warden court at Kelso. On the way, he visited Langton tower, near Duns, in order to settle an internal squabble of the Cockburns, when there appeared on the scene Sir David Home of Wedder-

* Bruised.

burn, a fiery character who was later, with the help of his brother John, to murder the Abbot of Coldingham. Wedderburn managed to pick a quarrel with de la Beauté, and a fracas ensued in which the French attendants beat off their assailants, and the warden made his escape. As his horse picked its way over the mosses, however, it stumbled and fell and, before he could remount, the Homes were upon him, hunting the wretched man like a hare until they finally ran him down and hacked off his head. Then, "because his hair was long like women's and plat on a Head Lace, David Home of Wedderburn knit it on his Saddle-Bow" and galloped off with his bloody trophy to exhibit it on a pole in the town of Duns. It has been slanderously suggested that it was the cavalier treatment subsequently accorded to the warden's head that inspired the games of handball that remain a feature of the Common Ridings there.

Neither this, of course, nor the affair at Ferniehirst, nor the occasional tortures and frequent mincings in which the Borderers indulged, were considered as being anything out of the way in those parts; but before criticizing them for their brutalities it might be as well to consider the times in which they lived. It was in 1602, for instance, that according to *Pitcairn's Criminal Trials* a lady in the Burnsyde of Saling, nowhere near the Borders, not only had her house robbed, but was literally grilled by the thief who "sett her bair erse upon a red-hot griddle standing on the fire, and held her perforce thereon".

Torture by the rack, the thumbscrews or the 'boot', into which wedges were forced until the foot was irreparably crushed, were, of course, a normal part of official procedure, and one against which there seems to have been small outcry. The sixteenth century, indeed, was little less rough and violent than its predecessor, and no whit less cruel.

In England, moreover, brutality, plunder and extortion were by no means unknown among people who should have known better, let alone the soldiers returning from the wars in the Low Countries. The goings-on in Scotland were even worse for, with some or other of the nobility almost permanently in revolt, the savagery of the private armies that they controlled probably exceeded that of the Borderers. It was indeed an age when physical pain was something to be inflicted—and endured

—almost as a matter of course. No-one, for example, seems to have found anything remarkable about the fact that on 17th March 1524, "Margaret Davy, a maid, was boiled at Smithfield for poisoning three households she had dwelled in".

If nowadays we are revolted by the barbarities that were practised in the name of the law, what are we to think of those that were perpetrated in the cause of religion? In England the burning alive of so-called heretics was considered a positive virtue, while in Scotland the dignitaries of the Church preferred to tie them to the stake by the neck and then to remove the stool that supported them, so that they slowly strangled, before being burnt. Patrick Hamilton, who was one of the earliest reformers, became the "first Scottish martyr and the best" when he was roasted alive on a slow fire in the most revolting circumstances.

With Calvinism there came to Scotland the witchcraft mania that reflected the situation on the Continent, where the slightest suspicion of witchcraft resulted in not only men and women, but children as well, being tortured in the most sickening manner, in order to extort the confessions without which they could not normally be convicted, and where those who had confessed might be slowly roasted on a red-hot chair especially designed for the purpose, before being consigned to the gallows. Imagine, also, the fate of Margaret Clitheroe who, in the year of Babington's plot against Elizabeth, was slowly pressed to death at the Tolbooth of York after being convicted of harbouring a priest. The reivers, then, were probably no more cruel than many of their contemporaries: their fault lay not so much in the way that they committed their crimes as in the fact that they committed them at all—or, at any rate, so many of them.

Most of the mutilations in which the reivers indulged, or which they themselves suffered, were probably inflicted in hot blood, so that the to-names they sometimes inspired were evidence of more or less honourable scars. Notable exceptions to this general rule, however, were one of the Armstrongs, known as Stowlugs because his ears had been cropped, as well as Jock Elliot, otherwise known as Halflugs. On the other hand, Nebless Clemy Crozier had no doubt lost his nose in a foray, as had Fyngarles Willie his fingers. Others in the same case included Hob-wait-about-him (meaning Hob-with-a-weal), John-with-the-one-hand and (most significant of all), "Thom Scott called the Stower", meaning the carver-up.

So much for bodily peculiarities. Another excuse for a to-name must have been the eccentricities of dress which differentiated some of the reivers. Will Bell, for instance, was known as Red Cloak, another desperado as White Cloak, and a certain Willie Elliot as Whitsarke (white shirt). Others bore the name of White Hose and Red Sleeves, while one of the Nixons was named Gowdy, presumably after something gold that he affected. Lance Armstrong was Bonnyboots, Elliot of Stobs was Gibbie with the Golden Garters, and a certain Hector Armstrong was Ekie Braidbelt. Or it might be the reiver's favourite weapon that marked him out from his fellows, as with Jock o' the lang brand (sword), Thom with the Lance, or an unidentified gentleman known as Braidswerd.

With the sarcastically named 'Mistress' Ker and another of the same surname called The Lady; with John Innes the Sweet Man and Davy Elliot known as the Carling, or Old Woman, we enter on another category concerned this time with character, rather than appearance. The fawning nature of Smys Thom, the bad temper of Dand (Andrew) Young called the Canker, and the woes of Unhappy Anthon were presumably inspiration enough for their to-names, as were the lady-killing propensities of Wanton Symie, Andrew Elliot the Wooer, William Hall called Wantoun Pyntill and Hob Johnston who was Goode at Evin, as well as the connubial shortcomings of a reiver known as Cold Fute.

The numbers involved in Border raids varied from two or three up to hundreds, and in the case of major battles between the different factions, thousands. Planning and executing a major raid, therefore, involved very considerable powers of leadership, and there is no doubt that such as the Bold Buccleuch, Gilnockie, Kinmont Willie, Wat o' Harden, Little Jock Elliot, and one or two of the Charltons, were possessed of considerable military ability in addition to their natural qualities of intelligence and courage. They and their henchmen would be distinguished by strength of character and awareness that have been commemorated in names like Hob the King, Dand the Man, Bauld Jock, and All our Eynds (breaths).

Sir John Forster once wrote to his superior that "we that inhabit Northumberland are not acquainted with any learned and rare phrases". "Refinement there was none," said a later writer, "and all the gentler arts were uncultivated and unknown". Perhaps this is less to be wondered at when one considers the state of the clergy and the extent of education in general. In 1578, for instance, there were only 21 schoolmasters in Northumberland, of which 11 operated in Newcastle, 7 in the other market towns, and only 3 in the rest of the county. In Cumberland, matters were nearly as bad, though in Scotland, as always, the standard of education was higher; if only slightly. In 1601, however, the accounts of the Edinburgh booksellers whose trade, of course, was not restricted to the Borders, showed that virtually none of the nobles and hardly anyone else except ministers of religion, members of Universities and a very few of the lairds, ever bought books. It comes as no surprise, therefore, to find that when Wat o' Harden married the Flower of Yarrow, the marriage contract was signed by the notary public on behalf of all parties *including five barons* "with their hands on the pen".

A reiver who was reasonably well educated, therefore, must have stood out from the pack, and this presumably explains such names as The Clarke and Lang Penman. But if so, why was John Nixon known as "No good Clarke" or, for the matter of that, a certain David as "Nagud Priest"? Possibly the latter had aspired to the priesthood and failed to last the course. Even the description of Andrew Ker as Tutor of Graden does not signify that he was particularly learned, but only that he was the guardian of the young laird of Graden.

Perhaps the most interesting of all the to-names, because of the challenge they now present to our imagination, are those describing past exploits. Dand Young, for example, was known as the Crooked (broken) Pledge, Archie Elliot as Fyre the Braes, George Nixon as Ill-drowned (and sometimes as Half-drowned) Geordie, and a certain Symon as the Foid (fugitive).

Less easy to explain are such to-names as "The Griefs and Cuts of Harelaw", given to a Graham (though it is possible that he had been a scourge of one of the Armstrongs), "Stand in the Rain" and "As it Looks".

CHAPTER FOURTEEN

Union of the Crowns

They shall beat their swords into ploughshares, and their spears into pruninghooks: nation shall not lift up sword against nation, neither shall they learn war any more.

Isaiah II, 4

So troublesome had the reivers become in the days of Henry VIII that he once conceived the idea "so to chastise those Borders" that he could "plant others in their places". He actually wrote to his royal cousin of Scotland suggesting that they should agree on some such plan, but nothing seems to have come of it, and it was left to James VI and I to try something of the sort. What would eventually have become of the Borders, had the crowns of England and Scotland not become united, it is difficult to imagine. During the latter years of Elizabeth, disorder had become so widespread that wardens were being forced, on occasion, to employ robber against robber. The reprieve, therefore, came only just in time.

The authorities were not the only section of the population to rejoice. The reivers, and in particular those of the West Marches, had convinced themselves that when the sovereign died, his or her peace was automatically suspended until the proclamation of a successor, and they determined to make hay during the short time that they expected the sun to shine. The few days that elapsed after the news of Elizabeth's death, therefore, saw the Borders literally in a blaze. The Earl of Cumberland was afterwards to insist that the Ill Week (or Busy Week) as this period came to be known, was instigated entirely by the Grahams. Armstrongs, Elliots and others, however, played their full part, as well as co-operating in the last really big foray in Border history, which penetrated as far south as Penrith, and involved the driving off of 1,280 cattle, 3,807 sheep and goats.

Now that the two countries were united, there was presumably no need of a frontier, together with all the garrisons and other paraphernalia that went with it. Soon after his accession to the English throne, therefore, James did away with the idea of separate Marches, and abolished the post of warden. He then addressed himself to the task of pacification; attacking the problem on two fronts. First came the psychological approach, which involved changing the name of the Border Counties to the Middle Shires. His second, and more practical, step was to set up a commission to administer the law.

First they ordered all strongholds in the Middle Shires to be demolished; an injunction that seems to have been carried out somewhat spasmodically for, while thirty or forty towers belonging to the Elliots were razed to the ground, some belonging to other surnames survived more or less intact. Perhaps it was in respect of these that the Privy Council of Scotland ordained that "all iron yettes" were to be removed and converted into "plew irnis"*. Proclamation was then made that all the inhabitants of the more obnoxious districts must "put away all armour and weapons" and keep no horse worth more than fifty shillings sterling, or thirty pounds Scots.

A further blow to the reivers was the disappearance of the Border Laws which, though somewhat rough and ready, had been far more acceptable than the ordinary law of the land which, as they found to their horror, they were now expected to obey. "If," for instance, "any Englishman steal in Scotland or any Scotsman steal in England any goods or cattle amounting to the value of 12d he shall be punished by death."

Meanwhile the rounding up of offenders went merrily on, speeded up by what came to be known as Jeddart Justice, from the number of reivers who were justified at Jedburgh, virtually without trial. The appointment of Sir George Home, now Earl of Dunbar, to take charge of the pacification in both countries, increased the tempo, if anything, and in September 1606, he "caused hang 140 of the nimblest and most powerful thieves in all the Borders".

By 1611, thanks to Dunbar rounding up and hanging such worthies as Mangerton, Whithaugh and Martin Elliot, the com-

* Plough coulters.

missioners were able to report that there was "perfect and settled peace and quietness" in the Borders; a statement that was not entirely borne out by the facts, for four months later another 92 reivers were brought to trial, of which 38 were executed at Jedburgh and Dumfries.

Among those who took to the task of pacification with enthusiasm was Lord William Howard, known to history, from the baldric he wore, as Belted Will, but to his contemporaries as Bauld Willie. The third son of the Duke of Norfolk, he had succeeded to the Dacre Estates and to Naworth Castle, by virtue of his marriage to the heiress who, on account of her great possessions, was known to all and sundry as Bessie with the Broad Apron.

Another, surprisingly enough, was the Bold Buccleuch. Nor was he the only poacher to turn gamekeeper. The author of the 'Diurnals', for instance, commented with unconscious irony, along with news of calves with two heads, a "pig with a gruntle on top of its head" and other marvels of nature, on the fact that various gentlemen of the Borders, including Scott of Harden and his namesake of Tushielaw, had met at Jedburgh to discuss how best to put a stop to robbery and violence.

Liddesdale and the Debatable Lands were together regarded by the commissioners as a special case, and it was ordained that the inhabitants thereof were to be removed to a place "where the change of air will make in them an exchange of their manners". Coming at a time when few reivers can have slept easily in their beds, this must have struck them as particularly ominous. Outlawry meant little to them, but transportation was something they had never envisaged.

Right at the heart of the storm rode the Grahams who had played off one side against the other till every man's hand was against them. First, the Commissioners selected for exile 149 of them, including William of the Mote, Richard of Netherby and John, who for some inscrutable reason was known as "All our Eynds"; that is to say, 'eames' or 'eynds', breaths. The question then arose where to send them. Eventually it was decided that they should join the garrisons of Flushing, Brill and other places in the Low Countries which, because they were held as security for a sum of money lent by Elizabeth to Spain, were known as the Cautionary Towns.

The government, however, failed to keep their promise to

provide homes for the exiles, and gradually the Grahams began
to re-appear in Eskdale and elsewhere. Such was the tide of
sympathy that greeted their return that the commissioners now
produced an extraordinary document signed by a number of
the Grahams, which concluded, "We therefore pray that we
may be relegated and banished as an evil colony to some other
part of your kingdom, there to spend the remains of our lives
in sorrowing for our offences". Perhaps they were so tired of
the brutalities of the Musgraves, Taylors and other agents of
the Earl of Cumberland that they thought almost anything was
preferable to remaining where they were. Accordingly, the
whole tribe; women and children this time included, found
themselves in Ireland, where they were expected to cultivate
the bogs and wastes of Roscommon and Connaught to the
advantage of the local landlords.

Next on the list were the Armstrongs, and particularly those
of Whithaugh. In 1609 a plan was hatched for the voluntary
settlement of Ulster in order to re-inforce the Protestant population, and great numbers of Borderers, feeling that there was no
longer any future for them at home, departed to try their luck
in Ireland. Many remained there to become honest, hard-
working citizens, and particularly to make their mark as
soldiers. Others drifted back, only to find, in the case of the
Armstrongs, that the Scotts and Elliots had been awarded their
lands.

There remained the outlaws, and it was James himself who
conceived the idea of rounding them up and transporting them
to Virginia, whence they would be hard put to it to find a way
back. In the end, this was found unnecessary. Instead, 120 from
Northumberland were sent off to fight in Bohemia under Colonel
Andrew Grey, and another 320 from Tynedale to fight in
Ireland under Edward Charlton.

Gradually those who had indulged in reiving on the grand
scale gave way to marauding bands of 'moss-troopers' that
haunted the wilder parts of the countryside, picking up a few
cattle or sheep as best they might, or stealing horses in England
to sell in Scotland and returning with the Scottish variety
rather than travelling empty. Violence, however, was a pastime
that died hard, and there are constant references during the
seventeenth and eighteenth centuries to the uncouth nature
of the Borderer, such as the description of the inhabitants of

Tynedale and Redesdale in William Grey's *Chorographia*. "If any two be displeased," he wrote, "they expect no law, but bang it out bravely, one and his kindred against the other and his; they will subject themselves to no justice, but in an inhuman and barbarous manner, fight and kill one another."

Gradually, however, the Borderers managed to find other outlets for their energies; one of them being in their spirited support for the Covenant. Like all converts, when they finally awoke to the realities of the Reformation, they did so whole-heartedly. As Cleland, himself a Covenanter, put it:

> For instance lately on the Borders
> Where there was nought but theft and murders
> Now rebels prevail more with words
> Than dragons do with guns and swords;
> So that their bare preaching now
> *Makes the rush-bush keep the cow.**

Preaching, however, did not always prove a satisfactory alternative to violence, as one of Cromwell's outposts discovered when Porteous of Hawkshaw and his men came upon them in Falla Moss, near the source of the River Tweed, and, coveting their horses and equipment, murdered all sixteen, one by one, and buried them where they fell.

Perhaps the last of the reivers, as distinct from the sneak thieves into which they finally degenerated, was Willie Armstrong of Westburnflat. Willie was quite unable to understand that the power of the law had at last penetrated to Liddesdale, and that other men's property must now be respected. Twelve cows from West Teviotdale were traced to his farm by their angry owners, who surprised him in his bed, bound him hand and foot and handed him over to the authorities at Selkirk. Here he was tried in company with those who had helped him to steal the cows, and all were duly sentenced to death. Seizing the heavy oak chair on which he had been seated, Willie broke off a leg and brandished it aloft, calling on his companions to fight their way out of the court. To his mortification, they would have none of it, only asking him to "let them die like Christians".

In fact, the martial spirit of the Border still survives, as witness the many great regiments, both regular and territorial,

* See page 90.

that it has produced; while smuggling, wrestling, hunting, horse-racing and rugby football have proved acceptable alternatives to robbery and violence.

Few men have caught the spirit of the reivers like W. H. Ogilvie in his 'Riding Ballad', which begins,

Last night a wind from Lammermoor came roaring up the glen,
With the tramp of trooping horses and the laugh of reckless men,
And struck a mailed hand on the gate and cried in rebel glee,
'Come forth! Come forth, my Borderer, and ride the March
   with me!'

I said, 'Oh! Wind of Lammermoor, the night's too dark to ride,
And all the men that fill the glen are ghosts of men that died!
The floods are down in Bowmont Burn, the moss is fetlock-deep.
Go back, wild Wind of Lammermoor, to Lauderdale—and sleep!'

No longer does the wind from Lammermoor invite the reiver to ride, and, in truth, "all the men that fill the glen are ghosts of men that died". Ghosts, that is to say, of members of the Riding Clans of England and of Scotland, who may have been, in Trevelyan's words, "cruel, coarse savages", but were also honourable in their own fashion, prepared to risk their lives in pursuit of a living; poetic, sometimes humorous, and above all brave. Those of us who bear their names, or in whose veins runs reiver blood, might have chosen ancestors of more virtue, but scarcely of more spirit.

BIBLIOGRAPHY

Among the more important sources consulted were the following:

Arber's English Garner (Tudor Tracts), Ed. Pollard, 1903

Armstrong, Rev. R., *The Peel Towers of the Scottish Border*, 1912

—,R. B., *The History of Liddesdale*, Vol. 1, 1883, and M.S.S. materials for a second volume

Bain, J., *Calendar of Border Papers*, 1894

—, J., *The Hamilton Papers*, 1890

Balfour, Sir J., *Practicks*, 1754

Bates, C., *Border Holds and Castles of Northumberland*, 1891

—, C., *History of Northumberland*, 1895

Black, J. B., *The Reign of Elizabeth, 1558–1603* (Oxford History), 2nd Ed., 1959

Borland, Rev. R., *Border Raids and Reivers*, 1898

Brown, T. Craig, *The History of Selkirkshire*, 1886

Byrne, M. St C., *Elizabethan Life in Town and Country*, 1925

Calderwood, D., *The History of the Kirk of Scotland*, 1843

Carlisle, Bishop of, *The Border Laws*, 1747

Cary, R., *Memoirs of the Life of Robert Cary by himself*, 1759

Chambers, R., *Domestic Annals of Scotland*, 1858

Charlton, Dr E., *Memorials of North Tynedale*, 1871

Child, F. J., *English and Scottish Popular Ballads*, 1905

Collingwood, C. S., *Memoirs of Bernard Gilpin*, 1884

Craig, R. S., *Hawick and the Border*, 1927

Crawhall, J., *Border Notes and Mixty Maxty*, 1880

Curwen, J. F., *Castles and Fortified Towers of Cumberland and Westmorland*, 1913

Dalyell, J. G., *Fragments of Scottish History*, 1798

Denham, M. A., *The Denham Tracts*, 1891

Dixon, D., *Upper Coquetdale*, 1903

Douglas, Sir G., *A History of the Border Counties*, 1899

—, Sir G., *Roxburgh, Selkirk and Peebles*, 1899

Elliot, G. F. S., *The Border Elliots and the family of Minto*, 1897

Fraser, G. M., *The Steel Bonnets*, 1971
—, Sir W., *The Annandale Book of the Johnstones*, 1894
—, Sir W., *The Book of Caerlaverock*, 1873
—, Sir W., *The Douglas Book*, 1885
—, Sir W., *The Scotts of Buccleuch*, 1878
Gairdner, J. (Ed.), *Letters and Papers, Domestic and Foreign, of the reign of Henry VIII*, 1880
Gauld, H. D., *Brave Borderland*
Graham, J., *Condition of the Border at the Union*, 1905
Heslop, R. O., *Northumberland Words*, 1892
Hodgson, Rev. J., *History of Northumberland* (7 vols), 1863
Holinshed, R., *Chronicles*, 1808
Hugill, R., *Borderland Castles and Peles*, 1970
Hume of Godscroft, *The History of the Houses of Douglas and Angus*, 1644
Jamieson, J., *Etymological Dictionary of the Scottish language*, 1825
Lang, A., *A History of Scotland*, 1924
—, A. and J., *Highways and Byways of the Border*, 1923
Lesley, J., *The History of Scotland, 1436–1561*, 1830
Lindsay of Pitscottie, *The Chronicles of Scotland*, 1814
Lowther, C., *Our Journall into Scotland, 1629*, 1894
Mack, J. L., *The Border Line*, 1926
Maitland Club, *A diurnal of Remarkable Occurents*, 1833
Major, J., *A History of Greater Britain*, Ed. Constable, 1892
Maxwell, Sir H., *A History of Dumfries and Galloway*, 1899
McIntyre, W. T., *Lakeland and the Borders of Long Ago*, 1948
Moysie, D., *Memoirs of the Affairs of Scotland*, 1760
Muncaster Papers (Hist. M.S.S. Commn : 1st report)
Murdin, W. (Ed.), *A Collection of State Papers*, 1759
Neilson, G., *Peel, its meaning and derivation*, 1894
Nicolson and Burn, *The History and Agriculture of the Counties of Westmorland and Cumberland*, 1777
North, Hon. R., *The Life of the Rt. Hon. Francis North*, 1819
Northumberland County History Committee, *Northumberland County History*, 15 Vols.
Oliver, J. R., *Upper Teviotdale and the Scotts of Buccleuch*, 1887
Pease, H., *The Lord Wardens of the Marches*, 1913
Pinkerton, J., *The History of Scotland*, 1747
Pitcairn, R., *Criminal Trials in Scotland 1488–1624*, 1833
Privy Council of Scotland, Register of the, 1880
Rae, T. R., *The Administration of the Scottish Frontier, 1513–1603*, 1966
Ridpath, G., *The Border History of England and Scotland*, 1776

Scot of Satchells, *A true history of several honourable families*, 1776

Scott, Sir W., Ed. Henderson, *The Minstrelsy of the Scottish Border*, 1902

—, Sir W., *Poetical Works*

—, William, *The Border Exploits*, 1812

Smout, T. C., *A History of the Scottish People, 1560–1830*, 1969

Spotswood, J., *History of the Church of Scotland*, 1668

State papers and letters of Sir Ralph Sadler, Ed. Clifford, 1809

Surtees Society, *The correspondence of Robert Bowes*, 1842

Thorpe, M. J., Ed. *Calendar of State Papers relating to Scotland*, 1858

Tomlinson, W. W., *Life in Northumberland during the Sixteenth Century*

Tough, D. L. W., *The last years of a Frontier*, 1928

Tranter, N., *The Fortified House in Scotland*, 1962

Veitch, J., *History and Poetry of the Scottish Border*, 1878

INDEX